The Craft of Fiction

Aber Creative Writing Guides

The Business of Writing

The Craft of Fiction

Ghost Writing

The Writer's Glossary

Writing Crime Fiction

Writing Historical Fiction

Writing How-to Articles and Books

Writing TV Scripts

Starting to Write

Writing Soap

Writing Science Fiction

Writing and Imagery

Kate Walker's 12 Point Guide to Writing Romance

Aber Self-Help

Choose Happiness

Write Yourself Well

Aber Money Management

Understanding the Numbers:

    the first steps in managing your money

Back to the black:

    How to get out of debt and stay out of debt

The Craft of Fiction

How to become a novelist

Jonathan Falla

www.aber-publishing.co.uk

ISBN: 978-1-84285-104-3

Website: http://www.aber-publishing.co.uk

The author's website is www.jonathanfalla.co.uk

Typeset by Vikatan Publishing Solutions, Chennai, India
Printed and bound in Europe

Contents

Preface   ix

Acknowledgements   xi

1   Introduction   **1**

2   Finding stories   **5**

Thirty six plots—or maybe twenty?   5

Journeys   8

Adventures   10

The misfit   12

Where to find such stories?   13

Moral dilemmas   18

Pitch your story to yourself   20

Summary points   22

3   Autobiographical fiction—the art of lying   **23**

Prepare to lie   24

Find your distance   25

Openings   27

Being truly miserable   29

Summary points   30

4   Storybooks   **31**

Look abroad   42

Summary points   43

5   Character, conflict, story   **45**

Character is fate—isn't it?   45

Gawain's dilemma   47

The conflicted protagonist   48

Public face, private conflict   52

A conflicted view of society   54

Incongruous traits and contrasts		55
Are novelists honest?		56
Summary points		58

6 Who tells the story?—voice, points of view, and tense — **59**

First Person		59
Second Person		66
Third Person		68
Which tense?		71
Summary points		73

7 Narrative structure — **75**

Three-act structure		75
Casablanca		78
The world		84
The coda		84
Varying narrative structure		86
Editing or developing your structure		87
Summary points		88

8 Research: Digging for truffles — **89**

The character of the times		90
Details do matter—sometimes		92
Digging for truffles		93
Some is dry as dust		95
Specialities		98
Talking proper		98
Summary points		101

9 Landscape, townscape, weather — **103**

Landscape and mood		103
Landscape and emotion		105
Landscape as situation and symbol		108
Groups in a landscape		109
Human resonances		110
Scents and sounds		112
Townscapes		113
Summary points		121

10 Interior design   **123**
  Sensory information   127
  The palimpsest and the museum   128
  Stock characters: libraries, labyrinths,
    bookshops   130
  Summary points   133

11 People portrayed   **135**
  How well do you know your characters?   135
  What do you give your readers?   137
  A matter of appearances—men   138
  Beautiful women   140
  Where—or when—to describe a character?   144
  Acts of kindness   147
  People and their little ways—using tags
    and motifs   148
  Giveaway moments   149
  Language and register   150
  A last thought on character   152
  Summary points   154

12 Fertile plots   **155**
  Mysteries and questions   155
  So: what is the question?   156
  Pacing the information   158
  Time frames   160
  Bookending   162
  Revealing the truth backwards   163
  Flashbacks   164
  Sub-plots and themes   165
  Twisting multiple threads   167
  Shocks   169
  Foreshadowing   171
  Summary points   174

13 Dialogue   **175**
  Register   175
  Conveying accent and speech types   178
  Conveying information   180

All dialogue is artificial   181
Lessons from film dialogue   182
Summary points   184

14   Fiction and film   185
Books for Hollywood   185
Camerawork: What are you looking at?   187
Authors of film and fiction   193
Summary points   195

15   Short stories   197
Why bother?   197
Some guiding principles   198

16   Editing   205
Edit stages   205
The broad edit (1): Re-structuring   206
The broad edit (2): Cutting content   206
The fine edit (1): Take it carefully   207
The fine edit (2): Economies of style   208
Stripping away redundancies   210
Why not cut?   212
Overcuts and damage   213
Reading aloud   214
Finding a friendly reader   215
Copy editors   216
The case of Carver   217
Style and taste   218
Presentation   219

Index   221

Preface

I once spent a year at the University of Southern California's film school. USC has close links to Hollywood, and they taught a very practical course that would equip its graduates to work in that industry. They were providing us (they said) with the tools of the trade. They were quite clear that employing these tools alone would not make for great writing; they were also clear, however, that without an understanding of basic techniques, you'd be unlikely to get far. In just that way, I imagine, the great painters of the Renaissance taught the apprentices in their studios that they might or might not have talent, but if they couldn't be bothered to learn how to grind colours properly, they shouldn't waste everyone's time with brilliant talk.

My teacher in Los Angeles, David Howard, sometimes quoted the Spanish playwright Lope de Vega.[1] Lope was the author of a huge number of dramas—possibly 2,000—who claimed to be able to take a new play from commission to first night in three days (one day to write, one to rehearse ...). Lope also wrote a book of instruction about writing plays, concluding with the advice that, when one had finished reading, one should lock his book away in a strong chest. In other words: study the skills of writing, absorb them, but don't dream of doing anything creative with a textbook on the desk beside you.

That is the spirit in which this guide to writing fiction is offered: something to read and consider and perhaps to consult as you work, but not to be followed slavishly. Please: do your own thing! But do it from a position of strength.

I have included numerous examples from literary fiction and also a good few from film. The examples are drawn from authors ranging from Chaucer (c.1385) to Orhan Pamuk

---

[1] Lope de Vega, dramatist, born Madrid 1562, died Madrid 1637.

(2010), from the anonymous 14th century master known as "the Gawain poet" to Jim Crace and Catherine O'Flynn, by way of Jane Austen and George Eliot, Thomas Hardy and William Styron, simply because these are all superb story-tellers—as are so many writers today. It's exhilarating to realise that we confront the same problems as were faced by Tolstoy, Cervantes and Shakespeare, and that novels published this week are employing strategies that were used five hundred years ago. So: relish this great tradition, and give it new life with your imagination.

My grateful thanks go to many friends and colleagues who have contributed their thoughts on this book, in particular: Michel Faber, Merryn Glover, Richard Le Page, Pat Lynch, Nessa O'Mahony, George Green, Anthony Warner, students and colleagues at the Moniack Mhor and Lumb Bank writing centres of the Arvon Foundation, and all those at Dundee, St. Andrews and the Open University who have helped me clarify my thinking.

Jonathan Falla

Acknowledgements

We are most grateful to the copyright holders for their kind permission to reproduce material from the following works:

A High Wind In Jamaica by Richard Hughes, courtesy of David Higham Associates. *A Writer's Reality* by Mario Vargas Llosa, courtesy of Syracuse University Press. *Being Dead* by Jim Crace, courtesy of the author. *Choke Chain* by Jason Donald, courtesy of the author. *Preface* and *The Vessel of Wrath* from *Collected Short Stories* (Vols 1 & 2, Vintage edition 2000 & 2002) by W. Somerset Maugham, courtesy of A.P. Watt Ltd. on behalf of the Royal Literary Fund. *Ignorance* © 2000 by Milan Kundera, trans. © 2002 by Linda Asher, courtesy of Faber & Faber. *My Son's Story* by Nadine Gordimer, courtesy of Bloomsbury Books. *Night Geometry & the Garscadden Trains* by A.L. Kennedy, courtesy of the author © 1990 A.L. Kennedy. *Night Train to Lisbon* by Pascal Mercier, © 2004 Carl Hanser Verlag Muenchen, Wien, trans. © 2008 by Barbara Harshav, courtesy of Grove Atlantic Inc. *Restless* by William Boyd, courtesy of Bloomsbury Books. *Sepharad* © 2001 by Antonio Muñoz Molina, translation © 2003 by Margaret Sayers Peden, courtesy of Houghton Mifflin Harcourt Publishing. *Shane* by Jack Schaefer, courtesy of Messrs. Peters French Dunlop © Jack Schaefer 1949. *The Crimson Petal & The White* by Michel Faber, courtesy of Canongate Books, Edinburgh. *The Falls* by Ian Rankin, courtesy of Orion Publishing Group. *The Girl with The Dragon Tattoo* by Steig Larsson, © Norstedts Agency 2005, English trans. © Reg Keeland 2008, courtesy of Quercus Books and Penguin Group. *The Master of Petersburg* and *Summertime* by J.M. Coetzee, courtesy of David Higham Associates. *What Was Lost* by Catherine O'Flynn, courtesy of Tindall Street Press. Every effort has been made to contact all copyright holders. In the event of any omission, holders are asked to contact GLMP Ltd.

1 Introduction

This is a book to have with you when you embark on the journey of writing fiction. That is not an easy journey, and it's as well to have a few friends and a toolbox along. It also helps to do some planning beforehand, and I hope to help you with that planning.

This does not mean that you cannot write without having made plans first, or without having worked out a plot outline, or without having a biography for your characters. It does mean, however, that fiction is a craft and a skill, and part of any craft is to have a clear idea of what it is that you are trying to achieve. Good novels seldom come of entirely free-flowing, unplanned inspiration; there are exceptions to this, but not many. The better your design, the more likely it is that the result will be good.

Think of a craftsman embarking on some fine furniture. To begin with, suitable materials must be found: if you are working from scratch, you go in search of the right timber—maybe into the forest. But you can only do that when you have a broad idea of the design, the scale, the proportions. Detailed drawings must be made, and you must work out how the joints will fit and be secured. Then the wood must be trimmed to size, allowing a little margin for error. When the thing is all fitted together, the processes of refinement take over: the smoothing, the decoration. At last comes the polish. It would be a ridiculous carpenter who cut a piece of wood and started polishing it before confirming how it fitted to the rest of the chair.

Not every writer works in this deliberate way; it may well be that your ideas only become clear as you produce first sketches. But there are crucial policy decisions to be faced, and as you make those sketches, you must consider the overall structure of your work. I asked a novelist friend whether he planned his work in advance. He said that so far he had always done so, but now—on his fourth novel—he was trying the new approach of starting to write without much plan, and seeing where it took him. This was someone with a highly developed literary sense, and some years of experience and success.

There are many things to ponder, apart from drawing up an outline; often the hardest part is moving from plan to execution, such that scenes and characters flow on through the text: novels need to be 'through-composed', as they say of romantic opera. We will take you through the following aspects of fiction, with plentiful examples. You don't necessarily have to absorb the chapters in this order, but there is some logic to it:

2. **Finding stories:** What makes for a good story? How to recognise a tale or 'true life' situation with potential? What qualities are we looking for? What about adventures, love affairs and other mysteries?

3. **Autobiographical fiction:** The pros and cons of writing from your own experience, and the need for lies.

4. **Storybooks:** A tour of some of the major forms of fiction, showing that all depend on different sorts of conflict and tension.

5. **Character, conflict, stories:** How does conflict in a character drive a story? What about 'conflicted characters'—people torn in different directions?

6. **Points of view:** A discussion of the strengths and weaknesses of the main writing voices, and also of tenses.

7. **Narrative structure:** Why do we need a structure? What are the essential structures of storytelling? How does three-act structure work? In what ways can this structure be varied or subverted?

8. **Research:** What is the purpose of research? What are its pleasures and perils? The problem of 'Brand name periods'. What must be accurate, and what doesn't matter?

9. **Landscape, townscape, weather:** Why describe a landscape? Symbolic landscapes, atmospheric landscapes, and scenery as a vehicle for tensions and emotions. Fogs and mists and sunshine.

10. **Interiors:** Creating and exploiting interiors for the benefit of the story.
11. **Portraits:** How to describe a character? How do characters reveal themselves through language and reactions? The dynamic use of character description, tags and traits.
12. **Plotting:** The components of a strong plot, including time frames, parallel threads, flashbacks, foreshadowing, shocks and surprises.
13. **Dialogue:** Differentiating characters through speech and register. Why is some dialogue convincing and other dialogue not? The different uses of dialogue, its pacing and control.
14. **Fiction and film:** The overlaps considered, with lessons and cautions.
15. **Short stories:** What are the particular requirements, compared to longer fiction? Some guiding principles of short fiction.
16. **Editing:** Issues of style, the benefits and pitfalls of economy. How much can be left out? Finding your own style. How to edit.

One thing must be repeated: nothing here constitutes a "rule". Tools, yes; rules, never. There is not a single recommendation in this book for which you could not find a counter-example working effectively in some specimen of fine, original fiction. However, you may also read a novel that you feel is somehow unsatisfactory, and when you examine it again, you might conclude that the author has not paid sufficient attention to some simple principle. If you consider the points discussed here, you will have a good understanding of the essential craft. What you do then is up to you—and I hope it involves subversion and risks: "You've got to go out on a limb sometimes, because that's where the fruit is."[2]

The emphasis in this book is on story-telling; the reflective aspects of fiction are much more difficult to prescribe but

---

[2] Will Rogers (1879–1935), American actor and humorist.

Greek classical tragedy and 19th century French works to build his list, which sets out very drily the main components of stories—the problem, the protagonist, the antagonist—and includes (for example) numbers:

1. **Supplication:** a persecutor; a supplicant; a power in authority whose decision is not certain.
14. **Rivalry of kin:** the preferred kinsman; the rejected kinsman; the object of their rivalry.
27. **Dishonour of a loved one**: the discoverer of the dishonour; the guilty one.
33. **Erroneous judgement:** a mistaken one; a victim of the mistake; a cause or author of the mistake; a guilty one.

If you recall classic stories or dramas, you will see how they correspond to these categories: consider (for instance) the plot of Shakespeare's *Measure for Measure* as an example of Polti's no. 1.[4] Whether or not you agree that all story situations are covered by Polti's catalogue, it is clear that each type involves human conflict. More recently, rival lists have been assembled: on the internet you can find, for instance, the *Twenty Basic Plots* of the Tennessee Screenwriting Association. But for all their differences, there is a common theme: stories need dilemmas, tension, conflict, difficulty.

Frank Daniel[5] defined the basic story as: *Somebody wants something very badly and is having difficulty getting it.* What "it" may be is infinitely variable: it may be freedom, it may be money, it may be revenge, it may be "the girl", or to save the planet, or anything you care to imagine. What is essential is the tension that this desire creates in your characters, and in those who are out to stop them.

If we wonder what *The Iliad* is "about", it seems inadequate to say, "it's about a woman, Helen, who leaves her husband for another prince, and how her husband comes after her." That hardly explains the Greek armada, the ten years of slaughter and heroism, the burning of Troy … or the story.

---

[4] If you don't know the story, there's a handy summary on Wikipedia.
[5] Frank Daniel was a presiding spirit at the University of Southern California. A noted Czech director, he taught *inter alia* David Lynch.

be a metaphorical trip: a journey to understanding, a voyage to self-knowledge, a long hard road to wisdom. It may be both a geographical journey *and* a psychological voyage. One way or another, the protagonist will be a changed person at the end; this is why actors demand to know: What is my character's journey? The change that characters go through may be described as a bridge, the from-here-to-there of personal change. This is often called the "character arc".

At the end of James's *The Wings of The Dove*, the heiress Milly Theale has indeed died, and for Kate Croy and her lover Merton Densher the question would seem to be: Did our scheme to trick Milly work? Has she made us rich? Milly has written Densher a letter, but neither he nor we ever get to read it; Densher passes the letter to Kate, who throws it unread into the fire. Then there comes a letter from the lawyers—but again, we are not told the contents. In the last pages of the novel, Kate and Densher meet in London—and it becomes clear that the subject of the novel is not really the money: it is about what Kate and Densher have done to Milly and to themselves. Here is the end of Kate and Densher's relationship, the last words of the novel:

> He heard her out in stillness, watching her face but not moving. Then he only said: 'I'll marry you, mind you, in an hour'.
> 'As we were?'
> 'As we were'.
> But she turned to the door, and her headshake was now the end. 'We shall never be again as we were!'

That is the journey that Kate and Densher have made: from what they were, to what they now are. And that is the story.

Don't forget the journey *not* achieved: the quest that fails, the vain flight for freedom that ends with the protagonist caught by their pursuers, or unable to escape a guilty secret. There is nothing more poignant, and often the picture is of someone who has tried to change, but cannot. Boris Pasternak's *Doctor Zhivago* includes a whole series of such journeys; its characters in revolutionary Russia flee this way and that, but are finally trapped. William Styron's *Sophie's*

Choice is a portrait of a woman emotionally destroyed by the experience of Auschwitz, but trying to put herself back together in Brooklyn, New York, in 1947. She gradually slides into alcoholism and despair but, just before the tragic climax, she attempts to flee south with her admirer Stingo who finds her in the last car of the train, drunk and slumped on the floor, murmuring: 'I don't think I'm going to make it.' But the story is not quite done yet.

Adventures

Journeys are adventures. In 1911, the German sociologist Georg Simmel published a celebrated essay called *The Adventure*.[8] An adventure, he suggests, is something that happens at the periphery of our normal existence, out at the margins of our familiar world—yet it takes on a central importance in our lives. It may be "adventurous" in the conventional sense of setting out for distant lands on an uncertain quest. Or it may simply involve an encounter. Medieval French poetry gave rise to a song form called the *chanson d'aventure*, which in English became the sort of folk song that begins:

> *As I rode out one May morning,*
> *I heard a fair young maiden sing …*

Seen like this, an adventure could be something quite still, and very personal. Think (says Simmel) of a love affair: this may be so far removed from our daily world that it almost seems to happen to another person; indeed, some people having love affairs use a different name. Our friends, our close family may never know that it happened, that we were "out there". And yet, this distant event affects our core being. We are never quite the same afterwards.

The 2010 novel by the Nobel prize-winner Orhan Pamuk, *The Museum of Innocence*, concerns a wealthy young Istanbul businessman. Kemal is well-settled in his privileged life and his circle of sophisticated and well-heeled friends. He is

---

[8] *Das Abenteuer.* The full text is available in English on the internet.

engaged to marry, his life set on a prosperous and happy path—until, buying a designer handbag for his betrothed, he meets an impoverished shop-girl, and falls in love. This chance encounter, this adventure, changes Kemal's life. He spends much of the rest of the novel on visits to the girl's family home—a poor world far removed from his usual milieu. He never tells his family or friends where he passes his evenings. He does not let his obsession enter his normal world; yet this peripheral life dominates his existence. The climax of the novel is a failed journey to Paris.

That fine old movie *Brief Encounter*[9] concerns an adventure, an adulterous affair that is never consummated. At the end, the woman returns to her husband who knows nothing of what has actually happened. But he suspects that something crucial has occurred in her life. He looks at her kindly and says: "You've been very, very far away. Thank you for coming back to me." Physically she has not been anywhere at all apart from the cinema, a friend's flat and a railway station, but she has been on a journey nonetheless, and just before she returns to her husband she almost throws herself under a train, and stands with the carriage lights flashing across her face—emphasising the inner journey she has made.

A last example: *Night Train To Lisbon* by Pascal Mercier combines many of these elements. The novel's protagonist is a Swiss academic linguist whose life is a model of order and discipline—until the morning that he encounters a woman seemingly about to throw herself off a bridge in the city of Bern. He intervenes, learning a little about the woman who is Portuguese. In fact, he never sees her again, nor discovers any more about her. But soon afterwards he drifts into a second-hand bookshop, and chances upon an old volume of essays in Portuguese that disturb and speak to him in startling ways. This man of rigid habit and study deserts his school post and takes the night train to Lisbon, attempting

---

[9] 1945. It was written by Noël Coward and based on his own play of the same name.

to track down the author of the book. His life is radically altered. It is a true *chanson d'aventure*.

> **WORK POINT:** consider some novels and/or films that you know well. How would you describe the 'journey' made by the central character? In what ways are they changed by the end?

The misfit

The key to your tale may be the protagonist's arrival in a new place. This is the "new kid on the block" story, the stranger in town who may be bad or may be good but will certainly leave things changed.

Here is a very compact specimen. This is the complete text of a story[10] by Robert Louis Stevenson—all forty-nine words of it:

The Citizen and the Traveller

'Look round you,' said the citizen. 'This is the largest market in the world.'

'Surely not,' said the traveller.

'Well, perhaps not the largest,' said the citizen, 'but much the best.'

'You are certainly wrong there,' said the traveller. 'I can tell you ...'

They buried the stranger at dusk.

There are several journeys here. Clearly, the traveller has made a journey to a new country, one that he does not understand too well. There is a journey which (it is implied) he *should* take: a journey of learning about others. There is a journey of personal discovery: he learns that he has made a dreadful mistake. Unfortunately for the traveller, he learns this too late—and makes a final journey to the grave.[11]

---

[10] Stevenson actually calls it a "fable".

[11] A friend reading this story reached the opposite conclusion as to what it was about: for her, it concerned the narrow-mindedness of citizenry turning to murderous xenophobia when faced with a challenge.

The traveller is a misfit. He desires to see the world and to cut an impressive figure in it, but only causes antagonism. Literature is full of misfits in every sort of setting: the sweet-natured young man amidst the brutality of a 19th century Royal Navy man o'war (Herman Melville's *Billy Budd*); the sane and independent spirit evading prison by hiding out in a mental hospital (Ken Kesey's *One Flew Over The Cuckoo's Nest*); the working class stonemason trying to enter the exclusive world of Oxford colleges (Thomas Hardy's *Jude The Obscure*); the sullen-tempered fisherman ostracised by Suffolk villagers (Peter Grimes in George Crabbe's *The Borough*); the extra-terrestrial alien abducting hitchhikers in northern Scotland (Michel Faber's *Under The Skin*).

The arrival of a misfit may have comic results: W. Somerset Maugham's *The Three Fat Ladies of Antibes* has the ladies on a slimming retreat in the south of France. They hate every minute of it but they battle to maintain self-discipline— until the arrival of a stranger who cheerfully eats cream cakes right in front of them, with farcical results. But the story of the misfit is very often tragic. Patrick White's *Riders In The Chariot* is to my mind one of the most magnificent and powerful novels of the 20th century; here the misfit is Himmelfarb, a German Jewish refugee who journeys to Australia and finds himself working in a bicycle lamp factory. The story is a replay of the Crucifixion.

The newly-arrived misfit may not realise what a chaotic figure they cut. Graham Greene's *The Quiet American* tells of a diplomat called Pyle posted to 1950s French Indochina, understanding little of what he sees, yet proposing to create a new 'Third Force' in politics. What Pyle actually creates is mayhem and death, upsetting the status quo and the lives of everyone—but he sees himself as a shrewd operator.

What all these stories have in common is tension, conflict, 'adventure', and characters making some sort of journey.

Where to find such stories?

In January 1872, Count Leo Tolstoy heard grim news about the household of a neighbouring landowner, a man called

Bibikov, who had dumped his longstanding mistress Anna in favour of his children's German governess. Heartbroken, and dismayed at her sudden social isolation, Anna had thrown herself under a train. Tolstoy, learning of this, had gone to the nearby engine shed where Anna's mangled remains had been brought, and he stared at the corpse. Out of this ghoulish curiosity came *Anna Karenina*. Notice that link with railways and personal journeys once again, as in *Brief Encounter*.

> **WORK POINT:** buy one copy of a newspaper—local, national, tabloid, whatever. Work through it systematically, and list the possible subjects for fiction. Don't ignore the business section.

Fiction writers develop an acute sense for a good story, alert for gossip or skeletons in cupboards, whether tragic or comical or inspiring, that feed the imagination. Our own families may be a fertile source: one of my grandfathers was an MP and lawyer who defended conscientious objectors in the First World War, at considerable professional risk; another ancestor was a sea captain in the Channel Islands in the 19th century who was drowned on his first voyage after his marriage ...

> **WORK POINT:** consider the history of your own family. What scenarios does it offer?

But such tales will make for powerful fiction *only if* we can identify the conflict, the tension, and some sort of voyage of discovery.

One of my students came up with the following notion for a piece of writing. His family were smallholders in rural Ireland, with a colourful bunch of cousins living nearby:

> My cousin Vincent has a disability; one leg is shorter than the other. Attached to the six-inch sole of his shoe are steel rods; these are fixed to a belt around his thigh. He wears long trousers to try and hide it. Vincent goes

to a special residential school. My father drives him up there at the start of every term. On the drive, we make a little pilgrimage to a holy well.

As Vincent gets older, he becomes reclusive. His sister, a nurse in London, takes him over there when he is sixteen. His lower leg is amputated and replaced with an artificial one. On his return home, he works on the farm until he breaks the artificial leg; this means returning to London to get a new one. They get broken frequently. His mother is constantly writing to the press and politicians about how unfair it is that her son can't get treatment in a hospital in Ireland. Eventually her plight is taken up on Irish national television. Vincent is outraged and warns her not to mention him or his leg in any more letters. She maintains her campaign regarding the lack of treatment centres for people requiring artificial joints. Two years later her photograph appears on the front page of the national newspapers at the opening of the new Prosthetics unit in Dublin.

This has potential for a most evocative piece. The question is: what is the nub of the story? Is it about Vincent's struggle for a dignified and fulfilled childhood in the face of disability? Is it about his mother's battle for justice with the Irish health service? Is it, perhaps, the conflict that grows up between Vincent and his mother, as she uses her son's disability as a weapon in her crusade, to his mortification? Or might the central story be something altogether different, suggested by that passing reference to the holy well: a conflict of faith and medicine? Whose story is it, and what is their personal agenda?

The task for writers is to look at the histories and scenarios we encounter, and to find the story in them. This may not be the obvious one.

WORK POINT: teasing out the story. Consider the following tale and find those aspects of it that make for a satisfying piece of fiction.

Here is another example of a family history. Indonesia (where I lived for a while, working for a publisher) is a country made up of several thousand islands. The story concerns a remote fishing community, a small, conservative society in a place with few facilities. This is a world where secrets are difficult to keep and morals are stern.

The story tells of a man called Agus, with a reputation as the best of the local sailors. One day, a ferocious storm sweeps through the archipelago, battering the forests, whipping up the seas and forcing the fishing fleet to stay safely beached. Agus is at home with his wife and three children, mending nets, telling stories and biding his time until the winds drop and he can start fishing again.

But there comes a knock at the door: his neighbour, a trader, is frantic for help. His little son is desperately sick with malaria, and there is no hospital here: the boy must be taken to the main island a short distance away. But, in this storm, there is no fisherman who is willing to risk the voyage. The trader has gone from house to house begging for help, but everyone has refused.

Agus looks round his own home, at the family that depends on him. He looks at his wife—and she gives him a silent nod of approval. He takes the child and mother down to his boat, starts the motor and sets out to sea. Against the odds, they make it across to the hospital—but the little boy dies anyway.

I heard this story from the sailor's granddaughter; she wanted to honour her grandfather's bravery by writing it up for publication. As we thought about it, however, we felt less certain. As a piece of biography honouring a decent man, it is clearly worth writing, but for the author of fiction, there is again that question: what exactly is the story about? Bravery, certainly—but is that enough to make it interesting? What is the conflict, and where is the tension? A journey is proposed and undertaken—but what personal dilemmas must be overcome, what personal journey must be made? The fiction writer needs to look beyond the bare facts and must now begin to invent, starting with these questions:

- Whose story is it? Is it necessarily the story of Agus the fisherman? Who else stands to lose—or perhaps to gain— from the situation?
- Does everyone support his decision to go? Who might oppose him and why? What about his wife and children? How might they influence matters? Are there cultural pressures, perhaps—a need for bravado?
- Is this the end of the story? What might happen next that complicates matters? Is Agus's journey in fact only the starting point?
- What moral, ethical or emotional dilemmas are involved?

The fiction author should look on a factual story like this as raw material—and be prepared to cook it. If you don't allow your imagination to get to work here, you may well fail to see the essential drama in a situation, and fail to make the most of its power. Agus's story may be treated in many ways:

- Suppose that Agus's wife does *not* want him to go. What if she says: you are the crucial support of our family, and have no right to put us at risk just because you want the glory of setting sail when other men do not dare. If Agus loves and respects her, what will he do?
- If he does *not* love and respect her, how will he sort out his feelings?
- Suppose that he is afraid to go, but she taunts him with cowardice? What if the household is not a happy one? Perhaps Agus's wife despises him as a weakling, and goads him into an action that is then catastrophic because he, the boy and mother all drown?
- Suppose that there are personal complications that others do not suspect. What if the child is actually Agus's, the result of a secret liaison? Does his wife know this? Is Agus going to risk his life—and jeopardise the legitimate children he should support—for the sake of his bastard? Will the rest of this conservative community find out? Maybe Agus comes to feel that drowning is the best way out for himself …

- Or suppose we tell this story from a completely different point of view: that of another fisherman who had been approached by the sick boy's father but had refused. Why did he refuse? Were his motives noble or craven? Suppose he was ready to go, but gave in to his family's fears, and now feels regret and resentment? Perhaps he changes his mind and rushes to the shore to help, but is too late—and he sees Agus's boat founder and sink? What would he feel then? What if he later loudly criticizes Agus for taking a stupid risk for a child that died anyway—but hears the villagers say, "Well, Agus proved to be more a man than you." What would he do then?

- In this case, perhaps Agus's boat journey is only the starting point for a much more complex story: *the story of the other fisherman*. The mistake this other man makes costs him his reputation and his self-respect. How can he possibly win it back?

We could continue this process, but you see that the bare facts of the story form only a starting point. What you must do is "look into it". You are looking for conflicts, tensions, and journeys in every sense.

Moral dilemmas

In Agus's story, we've looked past the facts to the moral dilemmas. Many works of fiction hinge on such a dilemma: an example is William Styron's *Sophie's Choice*, in which a young mother is sent to the concentration camp at Auschwitz together with her two young children. There she is confronted by a sadistic doctor who offers survival for herself and just one of her children. She must choose between her son and her daughter: one will live, and one will die. If she refuses to choose, all will die.

Let's look at moral dilemmas a little further.

Moral philosophers sometimes debate "trolley problems". This odd phrase refers to a class of problems involving trains (or trolley buses). The classic version goes something like this:

You are standing on a bridge over a railway line. Just down the line, you know that a group of seven men are working on the rails. You turn round, and to your horror you see a train coming towards you at speed. If you do nothing, it will kill those seven men. There is, however, something you can do: there is a set of points, and if you throw the switch you will divert the train down the siding and save the seven men. But you also know that there is one man working alone on the siding.

So, are you morally justified in throwing the switch? You will save seven men, but at the cost of deliberately killing one perfectly innocent person. Most people agree that this is justified.

But now, consider a complication. Suppose that there is no accessible siding switch, but there is another person standing on the bridge, a big man in a bright yellow reflective coat. If you push him off the bridge in front of the train, the driver will see and will slam on the brakes. Again, you will save the seven men at the cost of one life, but you will have personally, physically pushed an innocent man to his death. Does that still feel justified?

Or suppose you see a siding switch, but it is at the far end of the bridge. If you run to change it, you will knock the big man onto the line. His death is incidental to saving the seven workmen, a completely useless tragedy, mere collateral damage. Is it justified?

A "trolley problem" like this is remote and theoretical; the "you" character is abstract, and has no personality. As such, it would make a poor story, because there is no one to experience the agony of a real decision. How could you use such a dilemma as a base for fiction? The answer is: by giving the central character their own story. Suppose that you, the narrator on the bridge, know the one man working in the siding—and you hate him. Perhaps he once swindled you or sexually assaulted you. What if this fact is known to the authorities: would your story about the train be believed? Even if you were officially exonerated, what would the neighbours say? And if the facts are not made public, would you nonetheless be able to live with your complex guilt feelings?

By introducing a protagonist with personal conflicts, suddenly we have a story.

WORK POINT: devise a trolley problem for yourself, with all its variants. Then add the human story that makes it a worthy piece of fiction.

Pitch your story to yourself

Film and television writers are very familiar with the notion of "pitching" (as in: pitching a baseball). When you make a pitch, you get only moments to tell a prospective producer what your story is about and why it is interesting. In a few words, you have to grab that producer's imagination, so that they will pay attention, read your script and make your film.

Note carefully: pitching does *not* mean that you try to tell the whole story in three minutes. It *does* mean that you have to find the heart of the story, what we may call "the nub"—the nub of the matter. It is "what this story is about". My teachers in Los Angeles would say: If you cannot pitch your story in three sentences, you're in trouble.

A pitch may suggest a particular character faced by a particular moral dilemma, and a particular crux circumstance that forces him or her into action. Imagine, for instance, "the nub" of *Hamlet*:

> A young prince living in a claustrophobic castle feels disgust at his mother's marriage to his uncle. Then his father's ghost claims to have been murdered, and demands justice—but can the prince bring himself to resolve on bloody vengeance? Meanwhile, the uncle is becoming aware of his suspicions, even as the prince hesitates …

Not for a moment is this a profound critique, nor a full plot summary of Shakespeare's play. It is, however, a reasonably efficient "nub", identifying the motor of the story, and it is done in three sentences. It can be instructive to read the publisher's blurb on the back of a novel, because these blurbs are—at least for first editions of new novels—often drafted by the authors themselves. There, in a few sentences, you will find what the author considers the story to be about, and which aspects of it are most likely to grab your imagination.

Could you convey the nub of your own work? Could you pitch it to a listener in a few words, conveying the theme of the tale as well as its outline, without constantly backtracking or saying, "I should explain that …"? You need to be able to do this. As you embark on any story—and at regular intervals in the writing—be sure that you can say: "That is the nub of my story. That is what I am writing about." You may eventually change your mind, as other aspects or characters come to light. But (just to labour the sports metaphors): you must keep your eye on the ball.

Summary points

- Stories are about desire and difficulties.
- The effort to overcome these difficulties leads the protagonist on some sort of a journey, an adventure that will change them and their lives.
- The object of desire may be unimportant: the story may concern its pursuit.
- Adventures, misfits, and people suddenly out of their depth are typical starting points.
- There is story material all around us. The task of the writer is to look for the story in the material, to "look into" the facts.
- A story may hinge on a moral dilemma—but this dilemma must be experienced by real people.
- Pitch your story to yourself, and then to a listener.

3 Autobiographical fiction—the art of lying

The most hackneyed advice given to authors (apart from "show, don't tell") must be: "write what you know". This counsel is usually given to new authors, to beginners, as though later on they might be able to use their imaginations but had better play safe to start with. The advice may mean that you write about a place, a profession or way of life with which you are familiar—or that you write about your own life.[12]

Which is what many authors have done, but at different stages in their careers. Among frequently cited "autobiographical" novels is Charles Dickens' *David Copperfield*. Dickens' literary career began with a short story in 1833. Several novels followed, but it was not until 1849–50 that he published *David Copperfield*. By this time, Dickens had an expert's control on what he was doing.[13] For autobiographical novels, that is crucial.

There are several cautions to be made about autobiographical writing. The first is that it may be difficult to judge what in one's own life is worth inflicting on the public. I recall an old cartoon which showed two gloomy characters trudging along a dismal rain-swept beach. One says to the other: "I do think your problems are serious, Richard—they're just not very interesting."

There needs to be something more than the purely personal in the story; there needs to be a perceptible theme, an experience that others can empathise with, something of the universal that is illustrated by the conflicts and the events in your tale. So, are you able to stand back and look at yourself with sufficient detachment to perceive that?

---

[12] See Chapter Eight (Research) for a further discussion of "Write what you know".

[13] The full title is interesting: *The personal history, adventures, experience and observation of David Copperfield the Younger of Blunderstone Rookery (which he never meant to publish on any account).*

And then—recalling the tale of Agus the fisherman, and Vincent the Irish boy with the damaged leg (Chapter Two)—are you prepared to select from your own history in a sufficiently ruthless manner to get the best tale out of it, distorting or discarding whatever doesn't contribute?

Prepare to lie

Supposing that you do have a promising tale to tell: you must be willing to change and twist it to make a better story, even if that means veering away from your "truth". If not, you may have had an interesting life, but you do not have the instincts of a storyteller.

The screenwriting consultant Linda Seger wrote a well-known book called *The Art of Adaptation: Turning Life and Fiction into Film*. In the chapter headed *Why does life resist film?* she considers this question of manipulating true stories. There are, she remarks, many different narratives in any one person's life. However, most inconveniently, we do not lead our lives in proper dramatic order. In a good story, the threads gather together into one neat climax; in real life they frequently fail to do so. Often in reality the subplot will only crop up after the main story has concluded. Often there are apparently key personalities who just fade out of our lives and are never heard from again. The people who are most important to our day-to-day existence may have no role in the interesting story we wish to relate. Real life can be thoroughly awkward.

Seger describes how she was hired as a script consultant to look into the idea of filming the life of a famous country-and-western singer. She concluded that it wasn't going to work. There was an obvious climax to the singer's career, when he won a major prize for his music. But the love of his life did not occur until after that. There was no tension between the two—no suggestion, for instance, that his art might have jeopardised his love life, or *vice versa*. There was no conflict at all, and hence no real story.

All this applies equally to fiction. If you are not willing to re-order the story, then write your autobiography as fact, and don't bother with fiction.

The Peruvian novelist Mario Vargas Llosa gave a series of lectures[14] at Syracuse University (New York), in which he considered this relationship between fact and fiction. In the fourth lecture, he remarked:

> I am not saying that literature is something totally unconnected with reality. What I am saying is that the truths that come out of literature are never the truths personally experienced by the writer or reader. Literature is not a transposition of living experience. Real and important knowledge of reality always comes out of literature, but through lies, through a distortion of reality, through a transformation of reality by imagination and the use of words. That is why the novel that tries to depict real experience in a precise and objective way fails …
>
> Thus, when you write a novel you must not shrink from the idea of distorting or manipulating reality … You must lie without any scruples … because literature, in order to convince the reader, must become a sovereign world, independent, a world that has emancipated itself from its mother.

Find your distance

For the autobiographical writer, the problem is achieving sufficient distance from your own story to be able to view its strengths and weaknesses.

In my second novel, *Poor Mercy*,[15] I wrote about a time when I worked for an aid agency in Sudan. The Darfur posting had been a painful experience for me and for other expatriates involved in the famine relief operation. We discovered that we were helpless to influence events or the well-being of the people; we were the pawns of bigger players: armies, governments, rebels and international organisations. Meanwhile, our local staff suffered in ways

---

[14] The lectures were given in 1988. They are published by Syracuse University Press as *A Writers' Reality*.

[15] *Poor Mercy*. Polygon Books, Edinburgh (2005).

that were to some extent our fault. There was plenty of story material; there was high drama, there was death and danger, there was great tension. On the surface, it was a gift to a writer, but for several years I failed to achieve anything. I tried a film script; I planned a series of essays, then a book of stories. I could not, however, find the objectivity to write convincingly in the way that Vargas Llosa urges. The key turned out to be simple: I removed myself entirely from the story, so that there is now no one in the novel corresponding to Jonathan Falla. I was "writing what I knew" in terms of the landscape and the characters, the emotions and fears, the situations and dilemmas. But I had given myself the liberty to tell a far more compelling tale, and I felt free to alter the historical record. I completed the novel ten years after leaving Sudan.

Writers of autobiographical fiction have used many devices to deal with this problem of achieving distance.

J.M. Coetzee's *Summertime* is a semi-autobiographical novel (part of a trilogy) describing the young writer as he reaches maturity. He is an odd soul. The novel consists of interviews with five people who have supposedly known Coetzee at key periods of his adult life, interviews conducted and transcribed by an academic writing a biography of the famous author John Coetzee. There is a question to be answered: what is Coetzee like, and how did he get that way? Each of the interviewees gives a different account, and gradually a composite picture is built up.

Not every reader will be sympathetic to a novel in which an author seems so taken-up with him or herself. The precursor to *Summertime* was called *Youth*, and described Coetzee's life in London as a younger man in the 1950s. Unlike *Summertime*, the London novel is told as a simple third-person narrative, and thus—perhaps because there is no other character speaking—can feel rather preoccupied and unkind. The *Times Literary Supplement* reviewer remarked on, 'the oddity and lack of sympathy in this pinched and obsessive performance'.[16]

---

[16] Review by Peter Porter, *TLS* April 26th 2002.

The novel *Echoes of War* by William Rivière is another variant of the distancing process. This is a family epic spanning the First and Second World Wars. In many respects it is a portrait of the author's own family and home, but not in a way that you could call a factual record. The central character, Charles Lamas, is a distinguished portrait painter who serves in one war and lives through the next. There was no such figure in the author's real family, but there was a well-known animal painter (a Royal Academician) in the late 19th century. Charles is a compound of aspects of various men in the family, while themes and traits are represented by other invented figures. Rivière has transformed reality into fictional truth, as Vargas Llosa demands. It was, incidentally, Rivière's fifth novel, not his first, just as Dickens' and Coetzee's autobiographical novels came only after a succession of other fictions.

I do not suggest that you must always change everything. Certain life stories have that universal resonance from the outset, *and* a ready-made shape that works, because they already contain a build-up of tensions, conflicts and dilemmas. What is needed next is emotional objectivity, such that we see the issues that matter, not the obsessive minutiae. This requires detachment, and probably a gap of years. The novella *A River Runs Through It* by Norman Maclean[17] describes a father raising two sons in Montana (USA) in the 1930s. Both turn into writers, but while one works studiously at his profession, the other lives a wild life and runs into trouble. The novella is a largely factual account of Maclean's own youth and his own brother, but was written much later in life—it was published in 1976—when he was able to take a distant and calmer view of what happened.

Openings

Fiction will often wear a mask of autobiography. Here is an opening:

---

[17] Filmed in 1992 by Robert Redford.

> Squire Trelawney, Dr Livesey, and the rest of these gentlemen [have] asked me to write down the whole particulars about Treasure Island from the beginning ... [when] the brown old seaman, with the sabre cut, first took up his lodging under our roof.
>
> I remember him as if it were yesterday ...
>
> *Robert Louis Stevenson, Treasure Island* (1833).

If we look at the openings of novels and autobiographies, we see that there is a large overlap between fact and fiction. Here is how Dickens begins *David Copperfield*:

> Whether I shall turn out to be the hero of my own life, or whether that station will be held by anybody else, these pages must show. To begin my life with the beginning of my life, I record that I was born (as far as I have been informed and believe) on a Friday, at twelve o'clock at night. It was remarked that the clock began to strike, and I began to cry, simultaneously.

J.D. Salinger—in *The Catcher In The Rye*—dismissed with contempt such life histories; his narrator Holden Caulfield, attempting to explain his own state of mind, refuses to give us "all that David Copperfield kind of crap". It bores him, he says, and anyway, that sort of orderly autobiography is just the way his parents and other adult "phonies" would neatly account for everything—and it is precisely the phonies' way of thinking that Holden is trying to escape from.

One sometimes meets a nice parody of autobiographical openings. A fine piece of self-inflation begins *The Exploits of Moominpappa*, a children's classic by Tove Jansson; the eponymous Moomin describes how he is moved to write about his stormy youth, how he feels a tremble of hesitation as he picks up his pen, how he was found one bleak and blustery evening wrapped in newspaper on the doorstep of a Foundlings' Home, and how the warden who found him there picked up the poor little mite, looked up at the tell-tale stars and remarked: 'This will be no easy child. He's over-talented.'

Another farcical parody begins Laurence Stern's absurdist novel *The Life And Opinions of Tristram Shandy,*

Gentleman[18] in which the narrator claims to know not just what happened at his own birth, but even nine months beforehand, when the moment of conception was interrupted by his mother asking his father if he had remembered to wind up the clock.

Being truly miserable

A recent publishing phenomenon is the "misery memoir" or "mis-lit", in which an abused and loveless childhood is recounted. Bookshops sometimes have whole sections devoted to "painful lives" in uniform editions, with titles like *Little Boy Lost*, or *Please, Daddy, No*, or possibly *Raised On Catfood*. After glancing at a few of these, you may wonder who is being exploited more—the child, or the gullible public?

Some of these books have turned out to be fiction. One harrowing memoir by a mixed-race foster child in tough south-central Los Angeles was revealed to have been written by a white woman resident in a smart suburb (the publishers withdrew it). Another author sold millions and got himself onto the *Oprah Winfrey Show* where he was subjected to cross-examining and confessed that he had invented much of his "life". Should he not have just written the whole thing as a novel? (Would anyone have bought it?) Every autobiography contains more or less selection, interpretation and suppression of the truth. Often, the decision to call the book a "true life" or "a novel" makes very little difference to the text beyond a few name changes.

If you have decided to write an autobiographical novel, you will need to ask yourself where you stand on this point. If you are proposing to write fiction, remember that the claims of good storytelling must come before the claims of factual reporting. You cannot defend a poorly structured story by saying, "But that is what happened!" As Mario Vargas Llosa says: The writer of fiction must lie without any scruples.

---

[18] Published between 1759–67, *Tristram Shandy* is stuffed with false starts, irrelevancies and digressions, with one page completely black and another of marbled paper.

Summary points

- Can you stand back sufficiently from your own story to see the universal themes in it? If not, you may do better to extract yourself and fictionalise more thoroughly.
- Your life story may be fascinating, but possibly another participant in the same tale has a more revealing angle on it, one that will make for a better story. Never forget: it is your task to tell the best possible tale.
- There are many different ways of using your own life story; a first person narration may not be the strongest. It may be that other points of view are more revealing.
- Are you prepared to lie? To change the facts, the motives, and the order of events? If not, you shouldn't be writing fiction.

4 **Storybooks**

So—what sort of book do you want to write? A traditional romance with a beginning, middle and end? Something more adventurous? Something 'genre'? To help decide this, you will sooner or later need to decide: *What sort of conflict and what sort of journey am I interested in?*

It is striking that, after a period of experimentation in the early 20th century, the writing of novels has largely gone back to forms established during the 19th century if not before. Yes, we had 'stream of consciousness' and interior monologue in James Joyce and Virginia Woolf. Yes, there have been various eccentrics such as Samuel Beckett, Jorge Luis Borges and, more recently, W.G. Sebald who in remarkable books like *Austerlitz* combined strange discursive monologues with a selection of atmospheric old photographs. But the vast majority of novels published since World War II have followed the conventional forms, and this must be because these are proven story-telling devices, with structures that date back at least to the classical Greeks. We will look closely at those structures in Chapter Seven.

Let us consider a few of the major forms of fiction, and the sorts of book that result—not a comprehensive list, but an illustrative selection. It can prevent confusion and wasted effort if you realise that you are writing within a tradition, that you don't have to re-invent the wheel. Importantly, it will demonstrate that in most fiction, however varied, the driving force is still a conflict and a tension.

WORK POINT: as you look through the following examples, think of the varieties of tension and conflict they contain, and the very different journeys—real and metaphorical—that they involve.

1. **The Journey to a Distant Land:** This is still one of the most common forms of a pure 'adventure' in Georg Simmel's terms: something that happens on the periphery of our lives, but which has a central importance for us thereafter. You will be working in a grand tradition here: the modern English novel begins in 1719 with Daniel Defoe's *The Life & Surprising Adventures of Robinson Crusoe of York, Mariner.* The notion of somebody dumped far away and having to fend for themselves recurs in a thousand examples: *Gulliver's Travels*, for instance, or *The Country of The Blind*, a novella by H.G. Wells describing an Andean valley of blind people into which a sighted man stumbles. There is Joseph Conrad's *Heart of Darkness,* and William Golding's *Lord of The Flies*, and modern variants like *The Beach* by Alex Garland, in which a secluded holiday paradise in Thailand becomes a self-governing nightmare. Science fiction is full of examples since H.G. Wells' *The First Men in The Moon*, while cinema has versions from *Lost Horizon*[19] to *Avatar*.

These stories share a didactic, moralising tendency. The distant, isolated world allows for aspects of society to become exaggerated, for good or ill. Sometimes we see a utopia—as in the hidden valley of Shangri La in *Lost Horizon*—which points up by contrast the cruelties and hypocrisies of our own world. But sometimes, 'normal' values spiral out of control, so that in *Lord of The Flies* we see English schoolboys hunting each other down like savages. It is the tension between what we expect of society and what actually happens, the shudder of horrified recognition when we see the worst of ourselves revealed in a distant microcosm, that powers the tale.

2. **The Rashomon tale:** This is a format to try if you are interested in the slippery nature of truth undermined by conflicting interests. *Rashomon* was a film by Akira Kurosawa, released in 1950; I use the title as a label for stories that relate the same events from several points of view, offering markedly varied interpretations of the facts. In Kurosawa's film, a Japanese samurai and his wife are

---

[19] Based on the 1933 novel by James Hilton.

ambushed in a forest, the wife raped and the husband killed. We learn this story in the versions of the brigand, the wife, and a woodcutter who witnessed the attack, all of whom contrive to blame each other with wildly differing accounts of what happened. Then a spirit medium raises the ghost of the dead husband, so we get his version too.

This sort of storytelling goes back at least to Wilkie Collins' 1868 mystery *The Moonstone* in which several narrators (the butler, the lawyer, the poor relation and others) take up in turn the story of a stolen jewel, although they do not undercut each other quite as they do in *Rashomon*. Robert Browning wrote a long verse-novel, *The Ring and the Book*, concerning a true-life murder mystery in 17th century Rome. Browning has twelve narrators, including the Pope, the gossips of Rome, several comically pedantic lawyers, the accused and even the dying victim (a young wife), all giving their version. A fine modern example is Iain Pears' *An Instance of The Fingerpost*, relating murderously exciting events in 17th century England; each of the four narrators demolishes the account that went before. *The Successor*, by the Albanian novelist Ismail Kadare,[20] is based on a genuine mystery: the death in December 1981 of Mehmet Shehu, the anointed successor to the Albanian dictator Enver Hoxha. Shehu was found shot dead in his own locked bedroom. Was it suicide or murder? The novel relates theories offered by different players, including the architect of the house, the family doctor—and, in the last pages, the dead man's spirit summoned by a medium, just as in *Rashomon*.

A Rashomon story is difficult to write: the interpretation of the facts each character supplies must seem plausible as we read, or we'd have no patience with it, yet each one must be seriously different. The pacing of revelations must be carefully judged: the earlier accounts must not give *all* the relevant facts, or there would be no interest in later versions, but the first version must give enough facts to send the

---

[20] Winner of the first Man Booker International Prize in 2005. Kadare's novels appear in English in a double translation, having gone first from Albanian into French.

story on its way, and also enough such that later versions can contradict them. It is also difficult to maintain sympathy for the narrators and their points of view if they persistently undermine each other. For such reasons, a good Rashomon story is rare—but very satisfying.

3. **The epistolatory novel:** a story told in the form of letters between the characters: not so common in the twentieth century, but recently enjoying something of a revival. Many early novels were epistolatory, notoriously *Pamela* and *Clarissa Harlowe* by Samuel Richardson (1689–1761). Richardson's novels were very long, volume after volume of letters describing every detail of the domestic and emotional life of the heroine. *Clarissa* is at times very dramatic: there are duels, there is an abduction and rape in which the victim is drugged, there is a deathbed forgiveness, there is revenge … Everything is explained in long letters. Even as she dies, Clarissa finds the strength to write three or four letters a day, each of around ten pages … If the process sounds absurd, it now rather reads that way. But the epistolatory novel has strengths: few things reveal character, emotion and motivation as minutely as letters. This was Richardson's own reasoning; here is his preface to *Sir Charles Grandison*:

> The Nature of Familiar Letters, written, as it were, to the *Moment,* while the Heart is agitated by Hopes and Fears, on events undecided, must plead an Excuse for the *Bulk* of a Collection of this Kind. Mere Facts and Characters might be comprised in a much smaller Compass: But, would they be equally interesting?

Few forms so dramatically show hypocrisy and plotting at work; we may read a character promising a favour to one friend, while telling another that they intend something quite different. The tensions in the epistolatory novel are often between the surface and the undercurrents, between what characters honestly understand about themselves, and what we suspect from their language. And then we have the tensions that arise from "dramatic irony"—when our letter-writer explains matters in a way that tells us that they really haven't understood, or speaks about somebody in a way that shows they haven't grasped the other's motives at all. Our narrator may praise someone as "the sweetest soul I've ever met" while we suspect the other of being a manipulative brute. Or maybe our narrator curses someone we realise is actually being quite reasonable and innocent.

Burley Cross Postbox Theft (2010) by Nicola Barker plays with the conventions of the epistolary novel in new and comic ways. The story takes place in a pretty village in the Yorkshire Dales, where one night the postbox is forced open and the contents stolen. The local bobby investigates, recovering a stash of letters and discovering many strange things about life in the village, such as the reason that all the older males have suddenly lost their enthusiasm for their laptops and are now keen on buying stamps: there is a gorgeous new girl serving in the post office.

The epistolary novel is also receiving new life through new communications media. A student on a course I teach submitted a modern version made up of emails and text messages, interspersed with other documents. The result was a deft portrayal of a close relationship between two women temporarily separated in two cities—a paradox of distance and proximity, as the quick exchange of texts achieved an almost whispering intimacy.

> **WORK POINT:** construct an exchange of text messages in which one character tries to lure the other to an assignation that we know will cause them grief. Remember to use all aspects of texting: for example, which character is most fluently able to use text language? What clues will you give the reader that the victim misses?

4. The Diary: Usually comic, as in the recent cases of Adrian Mole and Bridget Jones, or (the classic Victorian example) *The Diary of A Nobody*.[21] Such diaries feature modest souls with big ideas, and the diary reveals character in ludicrous

---

[21] By George and Weedon Grossmith, first published as a serial in *Punch* and as a book in 1892.

ways the diarist doesn't intend. We see our hero resolving upon something magnificent that is obviously a waste of time, or something 'impossible' which has actually been done already. We see them stubbornly loyal to people who are obviously fleecing them. We see them repeatedly pick themselves up and dust themselves down in the face of setbacks in ambition or love, and there begins to be a quirky nobility about their pathetic doggedness. Thus, while there will be conflicts with other characters in the story, there is also tension within the lead character, as they seek the strength to carry on.

A modern form of the diary novel might be a blog novel, and there is no reason why an entire fiction could not be made out of blog entries showing a steady build of tensions. Look at this opening:

> I have just returned from a visit to my landlord—the solitary neighbour that I shall be troubled with. This is, certainly, a beautiful country! In all England, I do not believe I could have fixed on a situation so completely removed from society. A perfect misanthropist's Heaven—and Mr Heathcliff and I are such a suitable pair to divide the desolation between us. A capital fellow!

This start to *Wuthering Heights* could readily be a blog. Be wary of one point, though: a diary is generally a private form of writing, while a blog is, by definition, written for the public. The ways in which people reveal themselves in the two forms will not be the same. The diarist has no one to deceive but themselves—unless they are consciously writing for posterity. A blog may be a lie from beginning to end, or a pose, or a self-deception; the blogger may not have any idea of how painfully they give themselves away.

5. The Bildungsroman: This rather forbidding German term just means "novel of education", and usually describes a story in which a young character is taught the ways of the world. Early examples were mostly German, such as Goethe's *Wilhelm Meister's Apprenticeship*. Flaubert's *Sentimental*

Education has a young man learning the realities of love and politics in revolutionary Paris. Thomas Mann's *The Magic Mountain* is a massively dense and complex example: a patient stuck in a pre-World War One Alpine tuberculosis sanatorium is taught all sorts of lessons (including sex). Others are often more or less autobiographical, such as D.H. Lawrence's *Sons And Lovers*, and James Joyce's *Portrait of The Artist As A Young Man*.

The education is often a bitter one, the novel grimly ironic. At the end of *The Magic Mountain*, for instance, there is a sardonic recapitulation of what the young man has learned; he then sets off for the Western Front, where his new wisdom (and his recovery from TB) will do him little good. The hero frequently behaves rather poorly, and often ends up wiser but sadder, so there is a tension between what they would *like* to learn, and what they actually absorb. But they may also find a sort of freedom, escaping from a domineering mother in *Sons And Lovers*, or from the Catholic church in Joyce's *Portrait of The Artist*.

What might make a Bildungsroman today? Well: how about a nice English girl who wants an exciting gap year travelling around the world raising sponsorship money for an African charity—but who begins to have doubts as she sees aid at work, who finds her innocence and good intentions ever-more compromised in different countries, and who finally gets caught up in the hypocrisy and murderous chaos of international agencies and refugee militias in the Congo. That would be an education, certainly.

6. The Picaresque: Here the central character is a cynical adventurer who takes on the world and has a series of escapades. We learn of human folly and cruelty, and we cheer the rogue who outsmarts the establishment. Early novels were Spanish ('picaro' meaning rogue or scoundrel in Spanish) or German, such as *Simplicissimus* published in 1668 by Johann von Grimmelshausen, whose anti-hero wanders through the chaos of the Thirty Years War living on his wits and his luck. Grimmelshausen also wrote *The Life of Courage: The Notorious Thief, Whore and Vagabond*, another tale of the

Thirty Years War, in which the central figure makes her living by selling food to marauding soldiers and surviving as best she can—though her children are killed one by one. This is the story Berthold Brecht adapted for the theatre as *Mother Courage*.

The point of these stories is the portrayal of a rotten world in which only an amoral person can thrive—the sort of world recently inhabited, for instance, by Balman, the anti-hero of *The White Tiger* by Aravind Adiga, who cuts a cheerfully ruthless path through the hypocrisies of modern India.

Whereas in the Bildungsroman it is the hero who gets the education, in the picaresque it may be us, the audience, who are taught the lessons. *Don Quixote* wobbles around 16th century Spain on his skin-and-bones nag, encountering a series of misadventures in which he almost always comes off worst. There is little plot as such, nor does Don Quixote learn or change much; he is the same old fool when he dies as when he set out. The book is carried forward by its comedy and by its theme: the need to strive for justice in an unjust world, whatever the cost. That is the conflict and the tension.

7. The Historical Epic: sets characters against a tumultuous period of history, such as Napoleon's invasion of Russia (*War and Peace*). As I write this, a book with the subtitle *A novel of the Spanish Civil War* is being advertised; the description says much about the politics but nothing about the characters. Generally in epics there is a large cast, and the theme is usually that voiced by Rick Blaine at the end of *Casablanca*: "The troubles of three little people don't amount to a hill of beans in this crazy world." The tension, then, lies in a question: how to preserve your values when the only thing that seems to matter is survival?

Epics don't have to involve war. One of Patrick White's finest novels was *Voss*, based on the true story of an explorer attempting to cross Australia in the late 19th century. The plot is simplicity itself: Voss sets out, corresponds with a woman back in civilisation, hits trouble and dies in the outback. It is this simplicity which is regarded as part of its "epic" quality—that, and the grand descriptive sweep.

8. The Family Epic: You could focus your epic story on one family, and the adventures or misadventures of different generations. William Rivière's *Echoes of War* traces one family through the First and then the Second World Wars, showing how the values of these people—Norfolk gentry— are eroded in some ways, but firmly defended in others. In draft, the novel was entitled *The Burma Girl*: it was one young woman's life in Burma—including her capture by the Japanese, and her submitting to sexual exploitation in order to survive—that was the author's original interest. The changed title reflects more strongly the broader conflict theme of values besieged and preserved.[22]

9. Magic Realism: Although folk tales have always been full of magic, for a long time 'magic realism' was regarded as an almost exclusively Latin American preserve,[23] especially after a Cuban novelist—Alejo Carpentier—suggested that Latin American history was uniquely strange, 'a chronicle of the marvellous in the real.' Realistic story-telling is combined with the sometimes rather arbitrary insertion of magical elements: a woman trapped in a prison might suddenly sprout wings and fly out of the window. Or there's a surreal premise: one of Annie Proulx stories, *The Hellhole*, has just that: a hole to Hell opens up in the middle of a forestry track, into which various malefactors satisfyingly tumble. Proulx gave her first volume of stories an epigraph supposedly from an old Wyoming rancher: "Reality's never been of much use out here."[24]

It was the South American novelists, in particular Gabriel García Márquez and Jorge Luis Borges who gave the form

---

[22] But *The Girl With The Dragon Tattoo* was changed in the opposite direction (see p. 54).

[23] The term itself dates back to a German art critic, Franz Roh, in c. 1925, and to movements such as surrealism in painting.

[24] *Close Range: Wyoming Stories* (1999), and *The Hellhole* in *Bad Dirt: Wyoming Stories 2* (2004).

its greatest successes, such as *One Hundred Years of Solitude* and Borges's various collections of *Fictions*. Many European writers followed the lead; today, for instance, we think of Louis de Bernières in terms of his tragi-comic histories *Captain Corelli's Mandolin* and *Birds Without Wings*, but some of his earlier novels, such as *The War of Don Emmanuel's Nether Parts*, are pure Latin American magic realism; at the end of the latter, the besieged and threatened peasant community departs from the real world and makes its way towards a magical idyll. But this is not a triumph; rather, it is a retreat from a cruel world. In much magic realism there is an air of poignant melancholy, and a conflict between what we hope for—which is good, and magical—and what harsh reality will grant us.

Magic realism can be exhilarating, vibrantly colourful and very funny. It does, however, have an intrinsic problem to do with tension: if anything *can* happen in the story, then there is no compelling reason why anything in particular *should* happen. If, for instance, our heroine in prison can escape the firing squad by sprouting purple wings, then we need not greatly fear for her. If the baby tottering over the edge of a cliff is likely to be caught by an obliging giant moth, then why worry? One only has to think of supposedly magical and inventive films like *The Adventures of Baron Munchausen* to realise that, poorly handled, the fantastical can be very tedious.

10. The Panoramic Chronicle: This was a speciality of the Victorians, sometimes at wearisome length (as with Anthony Trollope) but sometimes with magnificent results; George Eliot's *Middlemarch* is one of my favourite novels, a broad canvas of provincial town life that contrives to be moving, exciting and morally complex all at once. A panorama will contain perhaps half-a-dozen major story threads which overlap but are also self-sufficient. The tensions portrayed are those that grip an entire society, including economic and class conflict, age *versus* youth, and modernity *versus* tradition.

A recent example is William Nicholson's *The Secret Intensity of Everyday Life*, a much shorter book but likewise concerned with half a dozen intertwined stories in one community, in this case the well-heeled middle-classes of modern rural Sussex. This requires dexterity in its handling, but is an excellent form if you are interested in multiple illustrations of a particular theme: Nicholson's theme is summed up by his title. The risk in a short novel is obvious: if you only have 70,000 words and you are interweaving half a dozen histories, then each one will only receive some ten or twelve thousand words, scarcely more than a substantial short story. This allows you little space for a subtle and profound exploration. With skill, however, the overall result—the development of a theme—can be surprisingly satisfying. A film parallel is the Richard Curtis comedy *Love, Actually* with its multiple romantic threads. The critics were divided, but it worked with audiences.

Any of these formats are available to you, the novelist, and there are plenty of others: genre fiction, sci-fi and crime, gothic and chick-lit. There is the novel-of-ideas which plays with a philosophical or scientific theme, such as those by Umberto Eco, Michael Frayn or Andrew Crumey. There is the anthology novel, a collection of short stories strung together by some device: for example, *The Secret Pilgrim* by John le Carré, in which George Smiley sits down for an evening of instructive chat with group of student spies, and we get a series of educational stories; or *Trainspotting*, Irvine Welsh's assemblage of tales about Edinburgh drug addicts. There are innumerable sub-genres, such as the "large tenement with all sorts of odd characters living in different rooms"; offhand, I can think of two 20th century novels, a Spanish play, and the film *Rear Window* that explore this scenario.[25] A skilful writer may take features of several types to create something new.

The questions for the novelist embarking on a new project are: "What am I trying to achieve, what conflicts and

---

[25] *Tenants of the House* by Gilbert Phelps, 1971. *Tommaso and the Blind Photographer* by Gesualdo Bufalino, 1996. *Historia de una escalera* (The Story of a Staircase) by Antonio Buero Vallejo, 1949. *Rear Window* dir. Alfred Hitchcock 1954.

tensions am I exploring, and which format suits this best?" Remember: a full-length novel—even just the first draft—may easily take you a year or more to write; I was involved with my own novel *Poor Mercy* for a decade, and much of the effort went into trying to find the right format for the material. Don't launch yourself on an ambitious project without giving thought to different approaches and formats. Look around, sample different techniques. And please …

Look abroad

Anglo-American writing is, on the whole, conventional and somewhat unambitious in its forms. I've mentioned the German novelist W.G. Sebald: although he taught (until his death in 2001) at the University of East Anglia, Sebald wrote in German and belongs in European traditions (the books are well translated and widely available). His combination of photo-illustration and discursive monologue is something not much found in English. Sebald's books inspire devotion or loathing or blank looks of mystification, but they are the sort of thing that you put down, and then sit, and think …

Antonio Muñoz Molina's work is equally inventive: one of the most highly regarded novelists in Spain, he challenges the conventions of form to great effect. His novel *Sepharad* (2001) is a blend of fiction, history, and memoir on the theme of exile. The result is funny, exciting, thought-provoking, and poignant.

Summary points

- Don't reinvent the wheel; many formats and fiction conventions exist already, and you can use all these, and subvert them as you wish.
- Old types of novel may be re-created in modern terms, both as regards language (blogs and texts, for example) and as regards changing society.
- Different novel types depict different sorts of conflict. Which are you interested in?

Character, conflict, story

Novelists are sometimes praised for their 'rounded' characters, or their ability to 'bring people to life'. Most readers feel that they immediately recognise certain fictional characters, while others leave us cold, seeming two-dimensional or unreal. We shall look in detail at the matter of portraits later (Chapter Eleven): but what importance does character have for the business of creating a story?

In Chapter Two we considered that formula: *Somebody wants something, and is having difficulty in getting it.* Previously we have concentrated on the "something". Now we need to think about the "somebody".

Character is fate—isn't it?

I once taught a fiction course with the novelist Deborah Moggach, who instructed the students: "Character is plot, plot is character." In other words: the story depends on the characters involved; similar circumstances would work out differently for different characters.

Is this true of life? It is often argued that "character is fate"—that a person's character determines what happens to them. Some believe that our fate is "all in the stars" anyway. Chaucer mocked this notion with his Wife of Bath, who outrageously excuses all her disgraceful behaviour by cheerfully blaming it on the planets that oversaw her birth:

> I always followed my inclination
> By virtue of my constellation.[26]

In one sense, the idea that our character always governs our personal story is clearly nonsense: the Jews who died

---

[26] *Canterbury Tales, Wife of Bath's Prologue* ll. 615–6. Originally: "I folwed ay myn inclinacioun/by virtu of my constellacioun."

at Auschwitz had little say in their fate, and their personal character made no difference to what happened to them *en masse*. But at an individual level? In his essay *The Art of Fiction*,[27] Henry James wrote, 'What is character but the determination of incident? What is incident but the illustration of character?'

This is the level at which stories work. There is a catchphrase in theatre: "*Acting is reacting*". Something similar is true of storytelling: a story consists of a situation into which a character is placed; we watch how they react. So, in William Styron's novel *Sophie's Choice*, within the mass tragedy of Auschwitz there is an individual tale of terrible moral crisis. In Roberto Benigni's film *Life Is Beautiful* the grim tale of the concentration camps is told again, but now the result is very different: the protagonist reacts to that situation in his own way, and helps his son to survive by making believe that it is all a bizarre game. The man's nature is warm and humorous, and the result is a comedy.

How else do we see character driving story? Think again of Henry James's *The Wings of The Dove* (see pp. 8–9 above), concerning the young couple in late 19th century London who wish to marry but have no money; they plan to trick the sickly millionairess Milly Theale out of her money by convincing her that the young man is Milly's true love. The story is propelled by the character of Kate—she finds herself in a situation (poverty) that she does not like, and she reacts by coming up with a scheme to get what she wants—and by the strongly contrasted character of Milly Theale with her wealth, her goodness, and her desire for life. Character drives the story entirely.

Another classic: *Madame Bovary*. Emma Bovary is a headstrong young woman who has rashly married a blundering country doctor. Sensuous, selfish and snobbish, she is very soon bored and frustrated, and she embarks on love affairs and extravagance that cause havoc. In another situation, Emma might have been happy—but trapped in a dismal marriage and in the narrow-minded tedium of a small town, her character reacts in ways that lead inexorably to catastrophe.

---

[27] Published in the collection *Partial Portraits* (1888).

In many stories, you will see how this holds good: someone is placed in a situation, and the story is a matter of how they react. It depends on what that particular character wants from that particular situation. One could put any number of different personalities in Kate Croy's position (*Wings of The Dove*), and get any number of different stories as a result. Character drives the story. It is dynamic.

> **WORK POINT:** consider some novels or stories that you know. How far does this idea of story—that it consists of characters reacting to a situation—hold true? If you were to interchange the lead characters between novels, what would happen?

Gawain's dilemma

A much older example is the medieval narrative *Gawain & The Green Knight*,[28] which goes as follows:

As King Arthur and his knights sit down to their New Year dinner, a terrifying figure enters the hall: a powerful knight, entirely green (including his horse). The Green Knight offers a challenge: he will allow anyone to chop his head off, here and now, if that person will come to the Green Knight's chapel and allow him to return the blow in one year's time. Gawain—an ambitious young knight—claims the challenge for himself. He swipes the Green Knight's head off with one blow; the Green Knight merely picks up his own head and rides off, telling Gawain not to forget their rendezvous. Later that year, the rather dismayed Gawain sets out to find him. After a long journey, he comes to a castle where the lord and lady say that he should rest until New Year, since the Green Knight lives nearby. Each day the lord goes out hunting, exchanging a promise with Gawain that whatever each may

---

[28] *Gawain* probably dates from the late 14th century, and has miraculously survived in a single manuscript now in the British Library, known as Cotton Nero A x. There is a theory that the author may have been one John Massey, but the work is usually regarded as anonymous. There are modern translations by e.g. W.S. Merwin (2002) and Tony Harrison (2010).

gain during the day, they shall exchange at nightfall. Each day, at the castle, the lady attempts to seduce Gawain and gives him a kiss—and Gawain duly kisses the lord returned from hunting in the evening. On the third attempt, the lady persuades Gawain to accept a girdle which she says will magically protect him from the Green Knight. Gawain does not give this to the lord. Finally, Gawain rides out to meet the Green Knight—with the protecting girdle tucked out of sight. He bares his head to the Green Knight, who swings a huge axe … and just nicks the skin on the back of Gawain's neck. That—he says laughingly—is because you were not quite true to our bargain: you didn't pass on the girdle (the Green Knight is of course the lord of the castle). It was all a set-up. Humbled and wiser, Gawain rides home to Arthur's court.

What part does dynamic character play in this? It is essential. Could this not be told as a simple plot, minus any characterisation? Yes, but it would have made only a very banal sense. What drives the story is Gawain's reactions to the developing situation. He volunteers for the challenge because he is vain, and because "his public" idolises him; Gawain basks in a reputation as the perfect young knight (though he falls over himself to pose as the weakest and most disposable person at the Round Table), and he wants to shine in this adventure. When he sets out, his dress and his horse are as glamorous as can be. At the castle, his behaviour is near-impeccable; he resists seduction (only just). But he is human, and he is frightened. When offered the chance of magical protection, he accepts it—and shows that he is not perfect after all. The whole story is a test of Gawain's character. The tension and the excitement lie in our wondering how he will react and cope.

> **WORK POINT:** suppose that Gawain was a coward, or a lustful seducer: what would happen to the story?

The conflicted protagonist

So, we see a conflict in Gawain's character: he (and his friends) believe him to be perfection-on-legs—but he is prone to fear, to love, to self-preservation. Frequently, stories are driven by such a conflict *within* the protagonist: think of *Dr Jekyll & Mr Hyde*. Such conflict may appear in many forms:

- Ian McEwan's *On Chesil Beach*: a young woman called Florence adores her new husband Edward but cannot bear the physicality of love. The marriage is ruined by a disastrous wedding night, and never recovers. Florence eventually comes to terms with this divide in her nature; Edward cannot.
- Thomas Hardy's *Far From The Madding Crowd*: the capricious Bathsheba Everdene is loved by three very different men: a dashingly reckless soldier, an educated and thoughtful landowner, and a stolidly reliable shepherd. Each appeals to a different side of her nature, and tragedy results from the clash.
- Orhan Pamuk's *The Museum of Innocence*: Kemal, a wealthy but weak-willed upper-class Turkish businessman, falls wildly in love with 'a little shopgirl', but cannot bring himself either to throw over the values of his own society, or to leave her alone.
- The film *Casablanca*: Rick Blaine is a tough, decent man who has fought for lost but honourable causes. But a bad experience in love has made him so bitter that he declares, "I stick my neck out for nobody"—until he is faced with the choice between his bitterness and his nobility: between saving the life of a wartime resistance hero, and regaining his great lost love who is married to that hero.

In each case, our divided central character would be all right, would "get away with it", were it not for a new situation in which they find themselves placed. Pamuk's hero Kemal could bumble along cheerfully in his upper-class Istanbul world, but he is hit by overpowering love. Florence in *On Chesil Beach* might have been quite happy to adore her young husband platonically—but marriage seems to demand sex. The more awkward the situation in which people find themselves, the more interesting the story.

They may also be faced with divided loyalties. After the failed reforms of 1968 and the arrival of Russian tanks in Prague, the Czech novelist Milan Kundera went into exile in Paris. Much of his writing (for example, *The Unbearable Lightness of Being*) has concerned the conflicting pulls that resulted. His novel *Ignorance* begins with a conversation in Paris between two women—one of them Czech—contemplating the newly liberalised politics 'back home' after the end of communism. Here is the opening:

> 'What are you doing here?' Her tone wasn't harsh, but it wasn't kindly either; Sylvie was indignant.
>
> 'Where should I be?' Irena asked.
>
> 'Home!'
>
> 'You mean this isn't my home anymore?'
>
> Of course she wasn't trying to drive Irena out of France or implying that she was an undesirable alien:
>
> 'You know what I mean!'
>
> 'Yes, I do know, but aren't you forgetting that I've got my work here? My apartment? My children?'
>
> 'Look, I know Gustaf. He'll do anything to help you get to your own country. And your daughters, let's not kid ourselves! They've already got their own lives! Good Lord, Irena; it's so fascinating, what's going on in your country! In a situation like that, things always work out.'
>
> 'But Sylvie, it's not just a matter of practical things, the job, the apartment. I've been living here for twenty years now. My life is here!'
>
> 'Your people have a revolution going on!'

These are the first words of the novel. Before we know anything else about Irena, we know that a new situation has created a dilemma for her. Her character is conflicted between the settled quasi-French career woman, with a Paris home and family, and her Czech-ness.

That's the starting point: a person facing a situation in which they feel drawn to do something which, because of their nature, will not be easy. They may not be at all sure about this (Irena has doubts about going 'home' to Prague), but they feel compelled. Or they may want it very much, but face great risks. Thomas Hardy's *Tess of The D'Urbervilles* begins with a family of country folk who get a mistaken notion that they are descended from aristocracy, and they try to recover that status. *Jude The Obscure* is another country boy with intelligence and a little education, whose schoolteacher gives him a longing to become a student at Oxford (renamed Christminster in Hardy's novel). Protagonists feel their present existence to be lacking: Emma (*Madame Bovary*) is bored to tears with provincial life; Gregorius (*Night Train To Lisbon*) feels constrained by his academic routine; Jude chafes at his lack of education. Then the situation changes; they are offered an adventure—and they seize it.

When people try to escape from an impoverished and limited existence, we may have every sympathy, but when their desire conflicts with their "proper station" in life, disaster often follows; Hardy's message is brutal: stay as you are, or face the consequences. Other people try to escape from their past: thus Conrad's *Lord Jim* hides himself away among remote island communities, hoping to erase a ghastly moment of cowardice; thus Jack Schaefer's *Shane*, a wild west gunslinger, tries to put that violent career behind him, attempting to become an honest farmhand. But when it comes to the crisis, the only way Shane can help the homesteaders is by reverting to his former self, the gunman. The mainspring of each story is the conflicted protagonist, their past, and their reaction to a new present.

The Czech drama teacher Frank Daniel described many character conflicts as "want *versus* need". Consider any shopping mall, stuffed with shops that will sell us whatever we want (fashion and gizmos) but nothing that we need (no milk or vegetables, no tools, no ball of string). In story terms, "want *versus* need" may describe the character who wants wealth and status, and will sacrifice anything and anyone to get these ... but who needs love and human warmth. Poor Jude, a humble stonemason who yearns for education, needs to face reality (as I said: Thomas Hardy's analysis is brutal). When he first applies to a 'Christminster' college, Jude receives the following reply from the Master:

Sir, I have read your letter with interest; and, judging from your description of yourself as a working-man, I venture to think that you will have a much better chance of success in life by remaining in your own sphere and sticking to your trade than by adopting any other course. That, therefore, is what I advise you to do. Yours faithfully,

T. Tetuphenay

One might see "want *versus* need" as "head *versus* heart". Think of the manager of a struggling company who knows that they should sack an incompetent junior but cannot do it, because the junior is attractive, sweet-natured and trusting. Think of the commander of an army besieging a town who cannot bring himself to order his artillery to open fire because he loves the local architecture (the nub of *Mudejar*, a story by R.B. Cunninghame Graham).

Public face, private conflict

Often the conflict in a character may spring from this: their nature is that which drives them to succeed, but at the same time makes their success unacceptable to society of the day.

Imagine a person who is both a pious Christian and a ruthless business manager, who exploits staff and destroys all rivals before going to church and sounding off about morality. I can think of modern examples, men and women. All is well as long as they are successful—but what if things start to go wrong, on either side of their lives? Mr Bulstrode, the banker in George Eliot's *Middlemarch*, is such a figure: his pompous piety creates resentment in his rivals, who use his not-so-Christian past to destroy him. Bulstrode's story hangs on these conflicting aspects of his personality, and on his desperate reactions to a changing situation.

Perhaps we all carry within us such incongruities and conflicts. In fiction, incongruities make characters warm, recognizable and sympathetic, even when they are the villain of the plot. This is important: without this, the reader will have little sympathy, or (worse!) little interest in their fate. Even Mr Bulstrode is a sympathetic character. He antagonizes his neighbours, but he is tireless in his efforts to benefit Middlemarch society. There is a crime in his past, but he struggles to make amends through good works. He can be mean to his relations, but is tender and loyal towards his wife. By the end of the novel, most readers will think of him as "poor Bulstrode".

We may meet characters whose behaviour is not what we would expect from someone in their position. They could be children. The boys in *Lord of The Flies*, stranded on a tropical island, turn wild, hunting and killing their companions. At the end of the book they are rescued by a naval officer who is puzzled and dismayed, saying that he'd have thought English boys could have put on a better show. From the outset, the children in *A High Wind In Jamaica* don't think as children should, certainly not as regards their parents:

> It would have surprised Mrs Thornton very much to have been told that hitherto she had meant practically nothing to her children. … it would undoubtedly have surprised the children also to be told how little their parents meant to them … Actually, the Thornton children had loved Tabby [the cat] first and foremost in all the world, some of each other second, and hardly noticed their mother's existence more than once a week.

We then see these ordinary children placed in an extraordinary situation—captured by pirates—and again they do not react as children should, but often show themselves to be selfish and callous. The plot springs from their behaviour.

Meanwhile, the pirate Captain Jonsen, far from being a vicious cut-throat, is a rather sweet-natured soul. In the trial that concludes the novel, the court and the public insist on seeing all children as good and all pirates as evil. Neither stereotype has been true in the story—but this public misapprehension of essential character leads to a tragic injustice.

A conflicted view of society

The conflict may involve the protagonist's own view of their position in society. Consider detectives: many crime novels feature detectives who are thoroughly conflicted, often melancholy alcoholics with a pathological inability to sustain a relationship or to take orders from their seniors. They represent the law-and-order establishment, but they are dysfunctional within that establishment. They work for the authorities, but mock authority. In their personal behaviour they can seem more like their criminal quarry than like their colleagues. But such a conflicted personality allows the detective to strip away hypocrisy and see fundamental values clearly, to have an insight into the criminal mind, and to feel a certain fascination with the criminal that keeps the detective passionately involved with the hunt. Such figures include Ian Rankin's permanently hung-over Edinburgh detective John Rebus, and Lisbeth Salander, the heroine of Stieg Larsson's *The Girl With The Dragon Tattoo*, a young woman from a traumatically abusive background who is, in turn, capable of vicious revenge. She is both at odds with society, and fighting to purge it. The original Swedish title of this novel was *Män Som Hatar Kvinnor* meaning, 'Men who hate women'. The title was changed for the English translation, shifting the focus off the crime and the theme, and onto the investigator; this was what the audience would find memorable: the conflicted character that drives the story.[29]

Rebus and Lisbeth Salander are hardly subtle characters, and their inner conflicts are raw. But such conflict can be finely drawn even in a detective. The 1960s Van der Valk novels by Nicolas Freeling feature a Dutch policeman with a taste for books and music (but without the snobbery of Inspector Morse), and with a stubbornly independent turn of mind that frequently leads him into a friendlier relationship with the criminal suspect than with the well-heeled bourgeoisie that they have injured. The way Piet Van

---

[29] Compare *Echoes of War*, p. 39.

der Valk investigates is governed by his remarkable ability to empathize.

> **WORK POINT:** consider a variety of crime novel investigators. How do the more modern ones—John Rebus, Kay Scarpetta, Kurt Wallander—compare with those from earlier works, such as Lord Peter Wimsey, Albert Campion and Sherlock Holmes? Where does the 1940s Philip Marlowe fit in? Which are the complex characters, and which aspects of their character propel their stories?

For many such characters, the personal conflict is between their desire to right a wrong that insults their notions of decent social order, and their disdain for actual social institutions. Imagine a different setting: a seafaring adventure, in which our hero is the captain of a Royal Navy frigate, passionately determined to fight the evils of the slave trade, but also contemptuous of the inefficiency, corruption and folly of his seniors in the Admiralty. Think of the trouble he will be in: even as he pursues the slavers, his seniors are on *his* tail, trying to bring him to heel. From the combination of these forces will spring most of the obstacles he must overcome in his story.

> **WORK POINT:** sketch a story in which a character with a mission is in danger of being thwarted by the very institutions that should be supporting him or her. These could be anything from the High Temple of Babylon to the police forces of a distant star (by way of the National Health Service, the New Model Army, a corporation or a trade union ...).

Incongruous traits and contrasts

Many characters are given behaviour traits at odds with their situation. Such traits can be quite simplistic: the sheriff of the small seaside town in Peter Benchley's novel *Jaws* (the source for the film) is frightened of water; this is a straightforward device for raising the stakes in new situations that he encounters. It can be a source of comedy.

A character may be given a trait that marks them out as an unusual individual in a particular world. Imagine a terrorist who loves singing madrigals—an incongruity based on our own preconceptions of the sort of person who becomes a terrorist, and the sort of person who sings madrigals. Rationally, why should anyone not enjoy any sort of music? But imagine the bizarre scrapes and conflicts this might lead to.

Such a distinctive personality conflict may be quite superficial (more like an identifying flag) or may be the result of moving into a strange society where the 'normal' starts to stand out. The heroine of William Rivière's *Kate Caterina* is an English girl who marries an Italian just before World War Two: hence the two versions of her name, and the basic conflict of her situation. Or it may involve more painful self-discoveries: *The Reluctant Fundamentalist* by Mohsin Hamid depicts a young man who carves a brilliant career for himself at US business schools and in the highest echelons of American high finance, only to find (after 9/11) that this is incompatible with his Pakistani background. The situation has changed.

You might also use paired characters with contrasting natures: think of 1970s British comedians Morecombe and Wise, or Peter Carey's *Oscar & Lucinda*, or many others. In *Sense & Sensibility*, Jane Austen sets up two sisters, one resolutely careful and guarded, the other passionate and excitable. The story highlights this contrast, and the reader's interest is held by it. Each sister's plot—love thwarted in various ways—is conventional, but each reacts according to their nature: towards the end, the sensuous and distraught Marianne allows herself to catch pneumonia—which her sensible sister Elinor would never have done—thereby provoking the crisis that resolves her story.

Are novelists honest?

A final thought: some novelists offer us an apparently evil character who is redeemed by a certain character trait.

A controversial example was Bernhard Schlink's novel *The Reader* in which Hana, a German concentration camp guard, is found to be illiterate, and thus perhaps ignorant of what was really going on in the Holocaust. Several critics objected that this is both thoroughly implausible—she'd have known anyway—and a poor excuse for carrying out atrocities. We may recall the old maxim: *Tout comprendre, c'est tout pardonner* (To understand everything is to forgive everything).[30] But if a novelist sets up an evil figure, and then pardons them by giving them convenient character traits, is the author playing fair?

In Chapter Ten, we shall consider detailed techniques for bringing our characters to life.

---

[30] Quoted by Tolstoy in *War & Peace*, but of uncertain origin. It appears as 'Comprendre, c'est pardonner' in the 1807 novel *Corinne, ou L'Italie* by the Swiss writer Germaine de Staël (1766–1817).

Summary points

- Think of character in fiction as a *dynamic* quality, driving the story in various ways.
- A story consists of a situation into which we place someone, and then watch them reacting in ways determined by their character.
- A conflicted character may 'get away with it' until a crisis or a new situation forces a choice—and begins your story.
- The more conflicted the character, the greater the obstacles they face, the more compelling the story that results.
- Remember: "want *versus* need".
- Conflicts and incongruities within a character are what make them sympathetic and interesting, leading readers to care about what happens to them.

6 Who tells the story?—voice, points of view, and tense

Who is going to tell your story? Yourself, in the First Person voice? Some all-seeing deity? Whose is the point of view? These fundamental questions have many consequences for your tale; each voice and point of view has its benefits and disadvantages, and many authors change their minds. Dostoevsky, for instance, originally wrote *Crime & Punishment* in the First Person from the point of view of the murderer Raskolnikov, but then re-wrote it in the Third Person. Let us recap the main voice possibilities, and consider some of the pros and cons:

First Person

The story I tell myself. There are two sorts: stories I tell concerning someone else, and those about me.

Here is a paragraph from a (non-existent: I just thought of it) novel called *On The Shore*, narrated in the First Person by an especially charming man:

> The boat's wallowing around like a drunk whore. I feel like rubbish, not concentrating—what do you expect? I've eaten damn all in five days, or drunk water for two. The front of the boat jerks up as it hits the shingle. I'm thrown forward, twisting my wrist painfully and banging my knee on the thwart which some moron has made with a sharp edge, which is pretty bloody unacceptable. I fall out into the icy surf and drag the boat up as far as I can, but I'm wrecked, for pity's sake! Staggering up the shingle, I move cautiously towards the tree line. I have to find that little prat Gibson, find where the keys are before he screws up totally.

But my head's spinning, I can't see straight, can't see
the fuzzy-haired savage in the trees and don't notice
the arrow until it's sticking out of my throat.

You notice that dying (with an arrow in your throat) is
not a problem; plenty of fictional narrators are dead, and
Orhan Pamuk's *My Name Is Red* begins with the words:
"I am nothing but a corpse now, a body at the bottom of
a well." Here you see some of the First Person narrator's
strengths and weaknesses. The narration can be strong, full
of immediate sensations, fears, impressions. We *feel* with
the narrator. We witness directly the tumult of emotions.
Characterisation is easy, because we can pile in the disjointed
speech patterns, the prejudices, the resentments. Notice
that a relationship is established between the narrator "I"
and the listener "you".

The drawback is that there may be a lot of information
that the narrator cannot plausibly know: where, for
example, is Gibson? It may take some contorted and
possibly clumsy tricks to reveal information necessary
for the plot—either that, or the narrator must stay centre-
stage throughout, which may be both implausible and
tiresome. You may even become confused yourself. The
Philip Marlowe detective stories, set in California from the
1930s–50s, are told in the First Person. In one of these,
The Big Sleep, a car is dragged from the sea with a dead
chauffeur inside. Neither we nor Marlowe ever work out
what happened here, and when someone asked the author
Raymond Chandler, "But who killed the chauffeur?" he
replied, "I've no idea".

This lack of knowledge has its uses. Any story requires
a question and some degree of mystery, and the ignorant
narrator may be searching for the truth—the point of the
novel, perhaps. They may be in the dark about the full
picture; much of *The Hound of The Baskervilles* consists
of letters from Dr Watson in the deep west-country to
Sherlock Holmes back in London—at least, Watson *thinks*
Holmes is in London (actually Holmes is very much closer
to hand). Ignorance creates poignancy and/or comedy when

the narrator is shown to be fallible, especially reminiscing in old age about events long ago, and getting them sweetly muddled.

Ignorance may raise the tension, and be a source of fear if not panic. It may be used in contrast with a more knowledgeable voice, for irony. Margaret Atwood's *The Handmaid's Tale* is set in a nightmare America where human fertility is failing. It is narrated in the First Person by a young woman used as a surrogate womb-on-legs by the tyrannical ruling elite. She attempts to understand, but inevitably there is much that she cannot know of what is going on in the world about her. The final chapter, however, is in the form of an essay by a future historian who looks back at the period of tyranny and sets 'the handmaid's tale' in context.

W. Somerset Maugham, in a preface to his *Collected Stories*, explained his own use of the First Person narrator, mentioning that it is a convention that dates back to Roman literature:[31]

> Its object is of course to achieve credibility, for when someone tells you what he states happened to himself you are more likely to believe that he is telling the truth … The *I* who writes is just as much a character in the story as the other persons … if [the narrator is] a little quicker on the uptake, a little more level-headed, a little shrewder, a little braver, a little more ingenious, a little wittier, a little wiser than he, the writer, really is, the reader must show indulgence.

An important caution there: First Person narration can seem smug, especially when used as the voice of someone solving a mystery. It is difficult to avoid an implication of "See how clever I am".

The First Person narrator usually has strong opinions about events. They may be angry and self-justifying, or regretful, or elegiac. This is an effective voice with which to

---

[31] *Collected Stories* 1951, Volume One. Maugham mentions the *Satyricon* of Petronius (c. 60 CE) and many of the *Arabian Nights* stories as early users of the First Person.

look back at an unhappy past and to seek some comfort or some understanding. *A River Runs Through It* by Norman Maclean (see p. 27 above) is like this; so is a well-known Scottish short story, *Night Geometry & The Garscadden Trains* by A.L. Kennedy. The narrator looks back at her marriage and the adultery that spoiled it, and she draws various conclusions, ending the piece thus:

> It is the story of how I learned that half of some things is less than nothing at all … We have small lives, easily lost in foreign droughts, or famines; the occasional incendiary incident, or a wall of pale faces, crushed against grillwork, one Saturday afternoon in Spring. This is not enough.

The First Person narrator could be an indignant ghost—in which case a continued pompous personality becomes comical. They may be snobbish, or cravenly inferior, upper class or downtrodden. The Glaswegian novelist James Kelman has, over four decades and eighteen books, developed a powerful voice for his narrators. They are generally Scottish, always men, and usually people on the fringes of Glasgow society: the drunks, the homeless, the jobless. This does not always endear Kelman to the critics; when *How Late It Was, How Late* was shortlisted for the 1994 Booker Prize, some were incensed that a string of Glaswegian profanities and bad talk should be rewarded; one of the judges (Julia Neuberger) threatened to resign, calling the book 'a disgrace'. But Kelman did win the prize. His position is clear: his characters have a story to tell as valid as any other, and he speaks their language.

By contrast, some First Person narrators can be superbly arrogant. Robert Browning's dramatic monologue *My Last Duchess* is told by a haughty Duke of Ferrara who tells a diplomatic visitor about his dead first wife. He recalls how her flighty behaviour annoyed him, and how he could have corrected her with a stern word, but did not: to criticize another's manners would itself be a petty, demeaning thing for a duke to do:

E'en then would be some stooping, and I choose
Never to stoop.

If you create a First Person with such a strong personality, you will need other characters in the story who are equally distinctive, to set against the narrator.

The First Person may just be a framing device, a simple means of beginning the book. In *Madame Bovary*, the story starts in the First Person, the narrator recalling his schooldays:

> We were all in the classroom when the head teacher entered, followed by a new boy not yet in uniform and by the janitor heaving a big desk ... .

The new boy is Charles Bovary, who will be Emma's husband. We learn little more about the narrator, and the First Person "I" recedes from the novel in a page or two. At the very end, however, in the last few sentences we have a hint of the narrator returning. They do not speak the word "I", but the story switches to the present tense and a renewed sense of a speaker telling us of recent events:

> Since Bovary died, three doctors have set up in Yonville one after another, and none has made a go of it, so quickly and completely has Homais outsmarted them. The pharmacist has a more loyal following than the devil himself. The authorities fawn on him, and he has public opinion on his side.
>
> He has just been awarded the Cross of the Legion of Honour.[32]

This First Person framing gives us an immediate way into the story at the outset, and a means of exit at the end. Even a conventional Third Person story—"The children entered the room and stole the jewel"—may include passing references to a First Person narrator. Richard Hughes does this in *A High Wind In Jamaica*; he inserts remarks such as: "Possibly a case might be made that children are not human either: but

---

[32] My translation.

I should not accept it." The effect is to give a warmer tone, and to increase our trust.

A similar device occurs in *The Museum of Innocence* by Orhan Pamuk, a novel of obsession in Istanbul narrated by the man in love, who grows sadder and sadder. In the last chapter the voice unexpectedly switches. Out of the blue, a new voice announces: "Hello, this is Orhan Pamuk!" This authorial voice widens the context at the end, comments on what has become of the protagonist, and prevents the conclusion from being too gloomily self-absorbed.[33]

Wuthering Heights has several narrators—Mr Lockwood, Nelly Dean, Catherine—who take up the story in the First Person and tell it to each other, with various degrees of scandalized relish. Such narrators may play mere bit parts in the story themselves: but they were there, they observed, now they report. If they tell their own story, they may have an ulterior motive for relating it. In Mohsin Hamid's *The Reluctant Fundamentalist*, the narrator is a Pakistani who greets an American stranger at a café in Lahore and proceeds to tell the visitor his life story. Excuse me, says the Pakistani, but may I be of assistance? He begs the visitor not to be alarmed by his beard. He assures the American that he loves America. He explains that, on seeing a stranger in town, he merely wishes to be welcoming and helpful. Everything is in the First Person, and the Pakistani narrator does all the talking; throughout the book, the American never speaks. By spinning his personal life yarn, the Pakistani contrives to detain the visitor in the café for a long evening—in fact, the whole novel—and gradually we realise that the American is by no means a casual encounter, and is being set up. This narrative trick takes dexterity; from time to time, the author Mohsin Hamid must remind us of the American's presence by, for instance, having the narrator say: "Ah, I see you do not like … [whatever]".

Just because your story-teller speaks in the First Person, this does not mean that no other narrator's voice can be heard.

---

[33]It is a coda (see Chapter Seven). We are being gently released.

You might, for example, show your narrator discovering a cache of letters or journals, allowing a contrasting voice from the past to contribute. In our work-in-progress *On The Shore*, our protagonist breaks into the home of his adversary Gibson, and shows up his own mean spirit in contrast with Gibson's humanity:

> Everything in the room stank; cleaning seemed to be beneath Gibson. The top of the paint-smeared bureau was stuck; Gibson being an utter slob, I was pushed to tell whether it was locked, or simply stuck together with oils or dried jam. But when I kicked it in frustration, the lid flipped down and spewed a fan of filthy paint-spattered notebooks onto the floor. I picked one up, flinching a little at the grimy feel, and read the first page that opened:
>
> *What then is nobility? Is it not possible that, even amongst the carnage I witnessed today, there was something fine? Certainly I've seen many tiny acts of kindness in the ghetto: people remembering their decency in the midst of an apocalypse. Is there not also, in this despairing insurrection, something stirringly magnificent?*

There are other variants on the First Person: for example, the 'stream of consciousness' used by Virginia Woolf, and by James Joyce in the final soliloquy of *Ulysses* in which Molly Bloom talks to herself in just eight vast sentences for some thirty pages, her thoughts tumbling out as they supposedly tumble about in our heads. This technique has its advantages—intimacy, certainly—but it has drawbacks also. It can be tedious to read, and its naturalism is entirely artificial. It tends to be stereotypic, the voice of sympathetic but unreliable, muddled or poetical characters. One rarely meets stream-of-consciousness applied to an icy-calm nuclear physicist.

A First Person narrator may be unreliable for many reasons. They may be a lunatic or a homicidal maniac, or just someone with an axe to grind, their account thoroughly untrustworthy. In one Agatha Christie novel (if you don't know which one, I won't say), the narrator turns out to be the murderer. In *An Instance of The Fingerpost* and other examples of the Rashomon story, we may not realise that a certain narrator is unreliable at all, until we read the next version and learn who the previous speaker was.

Second Person

I've re-thought the beach-landing episode of my new book *On The Shore*; maybe it will go better in the Second Person:

> You were in no condition for this, were you? You were no sailor, for all you put on a brave face. You hardly knew how to row; you were fooling yourself; when the boat hit the beach you fell flat on your face and yelped like a child. Poor you; if you'd known what was waiting behind the trees, you'd not have struggled up the shingle: you'd have climbed straight back in and headed out to sea, though Gibson would have laughed at you. As it was, you tottered like a drunk howling for anyone who might hear, until you were cut short by the barbed arrow that pierced your throat.

The difference of tone is obvious: it is now a mocking but ruefully affectionate commentary: *Poor silly fool ....*

This voice is particularly effective at conveying sympathy, or antagonism (*You stupid bastard!*). It can have the feel of an interrogator speaking very close to a victim or a suspect's face. It can reflect tension, panic and fear. This example comes from *Sepharad*, by the Spanish novelist Antonio Muñoz Molina. He is describing the plight of various undesirables in pre-WW2 Europe:

> You cross borders at night along smugglers' routes, travel with false papers on a train, and stay awake while other passengers snore at your side. You fear that the footsteps coming down the corridor toward you are those of a policeman. At the border, uniformed men who study your papers may motion you to one side, and then the other travelers, who have their

passports in order and are not afraid, look at you with relief, because the misfortune that has befallen you has left them unscathed, and they begin to see in your face signs of guilt, of crime, a mark that cannot be seen and yet cannot be erased, an indelible stain that is not in your appearance but is in your blood, the blood of a Jew or of a sick man who knows he will be driven out if his condition is discovered ... .

Notice that long last sentence, driving on and on, relentless and unforgiving.

In *Sepharad* and *On The Shore*, the detached narrator is speaking to the protagonist. But the Second Person narrator may be the protagonist talking to him or herself (as I do when I break a wineglass in the washing-up: "Wake up, Jonathan, you idiot!"). In this case, the voice will reflect all the tensions of the protagonist's situation.

The Second Person voice may, however, be a sort of disembodied spirit guiding and speaking to the reader, not to the protagonist. Michel Faber's *The Crimson Petal & The White* begins with this voice taking us by the hand and leading us through the squalor of Victorian London. This is the opening:

Watch your step. Keep your wits about you; you will need them. This city I am bringing you to is vast and intricate, and you have not been here before. You may imagine, from other stories you've read, that you know it well, but those stories flattered you, treating you as if you belonged. The truth is that you are an alien from another time and place altogether ... .

Here is a *frisson* of danger, although it is a tease—the reader is, of course, in peril neither from pimps nor potholes—and yet the author does want us to have our wits about us; he wants alert readers. The disembodied narrator both leads us through the action and also provides a commentary upon it. The voice continues throughout this long and playful novel, and at the end bids farewell.

There are disadvantages to the Second Person. Some readers find it confusing if it is not obvious who the "you" being addressed is: the protagonist, or the audience? When writing in the Second Person, you must be clear and consistent. Any change in the point of view—i.e. having a new disembodied narrator taking over the tale—is likely to be bewildering.

Other readers find the Second Person odd and wearisome, while others again feel that they are being told what to think and feel, and they dislike that. However, for a close-focus and emotionally charged story, and for a very particular sense of engagement, this may be a good, unusual choice.

> **WORK POINT:** imagine observing someone doing something difficult: defusing a landmine in Vietnam, cooking an elaborate meal against the clock, teaching a recalcitrant class. Describe it in the Second Person, speaking to the protagonist and discussing their feelings as they progress or start to panic and fail. Use a very close observation of their manner, facial expression and physical reactions to reveal their feelings under pressure: "You're trying to keep calm, but I can see your eye beginning to twitch …"

Third Person

I'm having another go at the beach-landing in *On The Shore*:

> When the forest people found the stranger, he was sprawled on the shingle with a long barbed arrow in his throat. They turned him over gently, seeing the emaciated limbs and sunken eyes. There was a ragged gash on his shin, and a cut on the palm of one hand. Of who he was, there was no indication—only, he was a foreigner, tall and blond. Nor was it apparent who had fired the arrow. One of the forest women called and pointed: a boat was drifting far out on the calm waters of the bay.

This is "Third Person limited omniscience"—a gristly bit of jargon meaning that the narrator seems to know much but not everything about what is going on. So, we don't learn who fired the arrow, or who the victim is: the narrator does *not* say: "The forest people did not recognise De Vere, and they did not guess that Gibson had begged Untawema to shoot him ..." The mystery is continued. Notice that this voice is capable of a distinctly melancholy tone, perhaps because we observe events but cannot assist, while our lack of complete knowledge puts us in their shoes a little, sharing their vulnerability.

If *On The Shore's* victim was named, and if full information about the hidden murderer was given, that would be "Third Person with full omniscience". This was the voice commonly used by the great 19th century novelists, including Austen, Dickens, and George Eliot. The narrator can give or withhold information, can hint at the future, can inform us of things that the protagonist doesn't know, and can comment ("If only he'd seen Gibson pleading with Untawema behind the trees!"). The story-teller is in full control, and may make a point of letting us know it. George Eliot cheerfully tells us what we should think. Here is the beginning of *Middlemarch*, Chapter 29, in which the author starts to speak about her young heroine, Dorothea:

> One morning, some weeks after her arrival at Lowick, Dorothea—but why always Dorothea? Was her point of view the only possible one with regard to this marriage? I protest against all our interest, all our effort at understanding being given to the young skins that look blooming in spite of trouble; for these too will get faded, and will know the older and more eating griefs which we are helping to neglect.

So this chapter is not going to be about Dorothea after all, but about her unattractive old clergyman husband Mr Casaubon. Chapter 37 is also about Casaubon, who attempts to govern those around him, and who now receives a letter telling him to mind his own business. Eliot instructs us to sympathise:

> Poor Mr Casaubon felt (and must not we, being impartial, feel with him a little?) that no man had a juster cause for disgust and suspicion than he.

Today, we might dislike the controlling tone of such writing, and the implication (very Victorian) that, while we should try to understand everyone's feelings, still there is one truth only. This voice can, however, give a satisfying feel of retrospective calm to a story, a sense that we have achieved impartiality.

A variant of Third Person narration is "Objectivity". Now we see everything, but are told little about feelings except what is clearly evident or can be gathered from what characters say. Events are described with care and clarity but without judgement or emotional involvement—although, if it is well done, we will feel engaged because we will understand the dilemmas and conflicts faced. Certain crime and science fiction writers use this voice which is particularly associated with Ernest Hemingway. A modern version of his stripped down, objective style can be found in Annie Proulx's stories in which the dry relation is ironic—since the events being described are often absurd if not surreal—and this has a delightfully comic effect.

In theory, a Third Person narration can move around among your cast of characters, seeing events from everyone's point of view in turn. In practice, this is often a weakness. The more different positions we take, the less we can build a strong impression. It becomes harder to develop tension, because there's no reason for anything to be concealed. It also becomes harder to feel rising emotions in any one character.

So: don't wander unnecessarily. Don't switch PoV in mid-paragraph without good reason. Don't give us half the picnic from Tom's cheerful standpoint, followed by two sentences describing how Dick felt uncomfortable with the family tensions, and then end the paragraph with Harry daydreaming about being somewhere else with his girlfriend—not unless you are making a point about everyone's disparate thoughts. Such writing is irritating, like a conversation constantly interrupted by the telephone; we can never settle into thinking about anything, and everything remains on a superficial level.

WORK POINT: the obvious exercise: take a page from a story and try changing it into different voices, including the Objective and a First Person stream-of-consciousness. What strength and weaknesses do you find? Which aspects of the scene does the new voice most readily highlight?

Which tense?

The next decision regarding your teller is: what tense to use? As with voice and PoV, try to avoid mixing tenses, even where you are clearly beginning a new section. Past and present tense narrations each have their pros and cons, and can have a characteristic tone as well. Here the main choices:

THE PRESENT (not surprisingly) makes for the most immediate writing, good for situations where a quick response is called for—either in the reader or the protagonist. Good for action sequences, for comedy, and for a character finding their way through a difficult situation; it gives a feel of suspense and tension—what will happen next? Turn the page!—but it is not so easy to use if you are looking for something more reflective, summing up experiences.

The present tense can draw the reader into an immediate involvement with the story. In Michel Faber's *The Crimson Petal & The White*, the narrator takes our hand and leads us into the scene, and we enter a real-time narrative that waits for no one.[34]

THE PRESENT CONTINUOUS ("She is coming towards me. I am throwing up my hands in dismay. I am falling …") can be effective in conveying a sense of unreality, or disbelief, or that surreal or dreamlike detachment of a person watching their own reactions. Again, however, it allows for no pause for thought, and soon becomes tediously hectic. Perhaps best used for short passages at the climax of an incident.

---

[34] This technique in Faber is discussed in Chapter Fourteen.

THE PRESENT PERFECT is the tense of recently completed actions, and as such is the first choice for e.g. a diary or epistolary novel, recording events day-by-day, hour by hour: "I have completed the first draft of the book, and I've posted it to the agents this afternoon. What a triumph! I've achieved something new here". Note also that it carries a *tone* of completion, of definite achievement, of closure. It seems to be saying, "I have brought matters to a conclusion". It also (and this is its comic and/or dramatic strength) sets you up for a reversal: "The agents have sent my book back unread! The utter fools!".

THE PAST TENSE is by far the most common, conventional tense for fiction, able to encompass almost any genre.

> **WORK POINT:** to appreciate the effects of different tenses, take a passage from a classic novel—something truly classic, like Tolstoy or James—and try putting it into different tenses, as you did with different voices. How does the feel of the passage change? Which authors seem most awkward, altered in this way, and why?

Summary points

- Each voice and each tense has distinct strengths and weaknesses. Before you choose, be clear what these are.
- Consider what you are trying to achieve with your story. If it is a mystery, for instance, then 3rd Person Full Omniscience is probably not the best choice, because the withholding of information will seem coy. For a reflective exploration of morals, however, or a panoramic survey of conflicts within a society, it might work well.
- What tone are you after? First Person and present tense are ideal for comedy, and can also do well with obsession and fragility. Second Person may be a good choice for something nightmarish and oppressive. Third Person (limited) may feel faintly melancholy, while full Omniscience can sometimes seem over-controlled … and so on. Experiment, and see what tone results.
- Beware of frequently switching PoV or tense without good reason.

7 **Narrative structure**

Any work of art needs a structure. Without it, a painting is a mess of colour, a symphony is a noise, a building falls down. In fiction, it is structure that allows the author to control the plot, to build the tension, to develop character, to hold our interest and to maintain that hold, so that we keep turning the pages. It is structure that gives the reader the sense that art has triumphed over the chaos of life.

Most readers, most of the time, will be unaware of the structure of a novel—at least, if the writing is any good. But they would soon know if there was none. So, what actually is narrative structure? Many will confidently answer that a story has a beginning, a middle and an end—but what does "a middle" look like, and what does it do?

Three-act structure

The most fundamental structure—in that it underlies a great majority of storytelling, whether fiction, drama or whatever—is generally called "three-act" and may be traced back to the drama of ancient Greece and the commentaries of Aristotle. In practice, plays or books may be organised into two, five or even seven acts, but the principles do not change and the essential components will be there, however it is divided up. At its most basic, three-act structure goes like this:

- the first act establishes a world, with certain characters, and a question or problem which they confront.
- the second act takes them on a journey or quest, and they wrestle with that problem and the difficulties they meet along the way.
- the third act concludes the plot with a climax, wrapping up the issues and answering the questions.

Let's look at this in more detail, to see the various components at work:

In **ACT ONE**, we are introduced not just to characters, but to a **world**. This may be a realistic world: Tokyo in the 1950s, a British battleship in 1810, Ancient Babylon or modern Madrid. It may be somewhere imaginary: a future colony on a distant planet, or a "lost world" in the jungle. It may be a prison cell, or even the inside of someone's head. But it is a world with its own consistent rules, an atmosphere and a history, a place where certain sorts of things happen.

In this world, **characters** are brought together: boy meets girl, or a villain meets a potential victim, or a team is formed. The circumstance that brings these people together is usually called the **catalyst**. For a brief while, we see them together; they begin to know each other, we get to know them and their lives. Then something happens, something dramatic that pitches them into a new situation, and which asks some big overriding **question** of them. The question may be obvious: Will they escape? Will they rescue the hostages? Will they save the planet? Will they win the trophy/money/boyfriend/secrets? Or it may be something more subtle, discreet and internal: will they survive an illness, or a betrayal, or some other time of psychological trauma? The adventure has now begun, and so this starting event is often called **the inciting incident** (or trigger).

In **ACT TWO**, our characters set out on their adventure or **quest**, hoping to reach their goal—whatever it may be. We watch them confront a series of obstacles, coming up with solutions only to find, just as one problem is solved, that another, sterner test arises. These moments are called **turning points** (or reversals), and Act Two may have several **sequences** each bringing us to such a turning point, at which the story sets off in a new direction with a new problem to solve. The stakes are raised, the tempo increases—but the big, over-riding question is still there: Will they escape? Will they find the treasure … etc.

Until we reach **ACT THREE**, Now all the mysteries have been resolved, all the doubts have been answered, and we come to the **climax**. Now, our hero at last makes a key decision and corners the villain. The case comes to trial, the victim confronts the fraudster, the coward meets the moment of truth, the "last battle" (of whatever sort) commences. There is only one question left: how will it all end? The end often involves a **twist**. These final events will contain a **resolution**, brought about by the protagonist, of the conflicts and tensions between the characters. There may also be a **coda**—a last short reflection, a new understanding of the world.

That is basic three-act structure as it is understood today. It contains within it the essential "story arc": world, quest, climax, resolution. You may be thinking: this is mechanistic and clichéd, and what has it got to do with novels anyway? But the more you look at storytelling in any form—from Medieval narrative poems to Hollywood blockbusters, by way of Shakespeare's plays and the major 19th century novels—the more you will find these elements at work, even if they have been adapted, subverted, or re-organised somehow. The novel may jump backwards and forwards in time. Not every component will always be there. But even in an experimental, innovative, multifaceted work, you may still find this basic structure underlying it. It is an exceedingly powerful story-telling tool.

Look back, for instance, to Chapter Five and the brief re-telling of the 14th century narrative *Gawain & The Green Knight* (p.47). The story arc and the three-act structure are very clear. There is the world: King Arthur's Britain. There are the characters brought together by the catalyst of a New Year feast. There is the inciting incident: the Green Knight's challenge. Then comes Act Two: Gawain's journey, its sequences of hazards and the series of rising temptations. At last, Gawain faces the Act Three climax, his meeting with the Green Knight, at which our questions are answered and the main issue is resolved. And, as a coda, a thoughtful Gawain makes his way home.

WORK POINT: sketch for yourself (one page of notes) a three-act story using all the elements highlighted above. Start with a poor baker's boy delivering bread to a castle in which a beautiful princess is kept imprisoned. The castle is the world, the catalyst is the bread delivery ... so, what sets the story on its way? What happens next? What are the turning points?

Here is a classic film example: *Casablanca*.[35] If you don't know it, get hold of a copy and watch it with some care to see how the structure works. Look closely at this detailed breakdown, and notice how the story as a whole is dominated by one over-riding question about Rick, while each sequence on the way is driven by a more immediate, subsidiary question.

Casablanca

ACT ONE

The world of French Casablanca in 1942.

Sequence 1: *What sort of world is Casablanca? What sort of things happen there?*

Desperate exiles throng the town. The French prefect Captain Louis preys on helpless refugee girls. Two German couriers are murdered, their "letters of transit" stolen. Many foreigners are arrested, some of them linked to the Resistance. At the airport, the Nazi Colonel Strasser arrives. Louis says, 'We shall arrest the murderers tonight—at Rick's bar.'

Sequence 2: *Who is Rick? What sort of man is he?*

Rick's bar, a popular place. Rick is a womaniser. But he has standards: he keeps a Nazi gambler out. He dislikes the murderous thief who stole the letters of transit, though he

---

[35] *Casablanca* started life as a stage play, which shows in its rather 'talky' script. The film was made in 1942, after the USA had entered the war, and some of its emotional power derives from the fact that many of the cast and extras were emigré Europeans for whom the melodrama of the film was only too real. Watch their faces as they sing the *Marseillaise*!

agrees to hide the letters inside the bar piano. But when the thief is arrested, Rick won't help: 'I stick my neck out for no one'.

Rick is introduced to Colonel Strasser and plays it cool. He is sternly warned: a famous Resistance leader, Victor Laszlo, is coming to Casablanca, hoping to escape to America. On no account should Rick try to help Laszlo—or the lady travelling with him. But Rick has no intention of helping anyone …

THE MAIN QUESTION: will Rick overcome his selfish bitterness and help Victor Laszlo and Ilsa?

ACT TWO

Sequence 3: *Why is Laszlo going to be a problem for Rick? Is it because of Ilsa?*

Into Rick's bar walk Victor Laszlo … and the beautiful Ilsa Lunde. Captain Louis, the French prefect of police, welcomes them cordially. Colonel Strasser and Laszlo confront each other coldly. Meanwhile, Ilsa greets the pianist Sam as an old friend. She asks him to play a favourite song, *As Time Goes By*. Hearing this, Rick approaches angrily, saying, 'I told you never to play that …'—and Rick and Ilsa come face to face.

Sequence 4: *What is making Rick so bitter?*

A flashback to Paris, to Rick and Ilsa madly in love and listening to *As Time Goes By*. Then the Germans defeat the French and reach Paris. Rick, Ilsa and Sam the pianist decide to flee on the final train—but Ilsa never comes to the station. She sends a note saying that she cannot. Shocked and heartbroken, Rick is dragged onto the train by Sam.

Sequence 5: *Can Laszlo find a visa, and escape?*

In Casablanca, Laszlo and Ilsa meet Strasser at the prefect's office. They are told that Laszlo will be dead, very soon, if he attempts to escape. Back out in the streets, Laszlo and Ilsa try to buy forged or stolen visas, but no one can help them. They are told: Rick may have those letters of transit; try him. Ilsa goes to Rick and begs for his help. He refuses: 'I'll do nothing to help you and your new boyfriend'. Angrily, Ilsa tells Rick that Laszlo is her husband—and was, even back in Paris.

Sequence 6: *Has Rick no decency in his heart?*

Rick is put on the spot: Laszlo's safety is desperately important to the free world. Won't Rick help? He refuses. Meanwhile, a young Bulgarian couple need help too—and Rick contrives a generous trick to assist them to escape. Then the Nazis take over his bar, singing loud military songs. To counter them, Laszlo inspires everyone else to sing the Marseillaise—and Rick allows this. The moment is wonderfully stirring, but the Nazis have the bar closed down. Rick has "stuck his neck out" for other people twice.

Sequence 7: *Can Ilsa force Rick to help?*

Late at night, when Laszlo is at a Resistance meeting, Ilsa comes to Rick and attempts to persuade him to give her the letters, then to force him at gunpoint. It is no good: they stop pretending and give way to their love. Ilsa explains the dilemma she faced in Paris (she had believed Laszlo was dead, but then learned otherwise). Rick understands—and decides to help. But how?

ACT THREE

Sequence 8: *Exactly how will Rick help—and who?*

Rick produces the letters of transit. By a series of devious tricks, he manoeuvres Laszlo and Ilsa to the dark, foggy airport, where a plane is leaving. Colonel Strasser pursues them and tries to stop the plane—but Rick shoots him. Who will board the plane? Rick convinces Ilsa that she must be true to Laszlo—and they depart. Rick and Louis leave Casablanca for a new life elsewhere.

THE END

This is three-act structure working very efficiently. You will note all the same elements: the world established, the catalyst and inciting incident, the series of turning points and new problems overcome, the rising tension, a climax, even a little coda as Rick and Louis walk away through the fog. You can see how each sequence has its own question and its own shape, building towards its own climactic moment (Rick receiving a stern warning from Colonel Strasser; Rick in shock at the railway station; Ilsa telling Rick that she is married ...). Not every structural element is in exactly the same position in *Casablanca* as it was in *Gawain*: we only encounter Rick in the second sequence. And you might argue that Act Two only begins when Rick, Laszlo and Ilsa meet. Nonetheless, it is all there.

So, that is Hollywood. But does this hold true of novels? Yes, frequently: this is, for instance, precisely the structure of that most careful and moral of novels, Jane Austen's *Mansfield Park*, in which all these elements (world, catalyst, inciting incident, sequences, turning points etc.) can be seen at work. And modern novels? Reading Orhan Pamuk's (2010) Istanbul story *The Museum of Innocence*, I was engrossed by the poignant love, the wit and ironies, the remarkable evocation of Turkish life and characters. I was not particularly conscious of structure. However, as I read I pencilled onto the flyleaf an outline of each section; looking back at my notes now, the three-act structure is all there, clear and complete with a coda.

Here is another condensed outline. This is *The Pickup*, a novel by the Nobel Prize-winning South African novelist Nadine Gordimer. It is set in post-Apartheid South Africa and a neighbouring country (not named, but perhaps Mozambique). I shall set out the basic elements of the story in what is sometimes called a "step outline".

> **WORK POINT:** look carefully at this outline, and identify the structural elements: world, catalyst, inciting incident, act divisions, turning points, climax, coda. Mark where they occur.

The Pickup

1. A car breaks down, causing a traffic jam in Johannesburg. A black mechanic, Ibrahim, comes to assist a white girl, Julie.

2. Julie is a rich South African. She has a vacuous job in PR and a circle of well-meaning but shallow white friends. Julie likes her "freedom".

3. But Ibrahim is an illegal immigrant, for whom the mechanic's life is a much more serious matter; it is his means of survival.

4. Julie and Ibrahim fall in love. He's clever and ambitious. They have a passionate affair, and he moves into her cottage with her.

5. A bombshell in the post: the authorities know about Ibrahim. He must get out, back to his poor, no-hope homeland.

6. Ibrahim fights to stay in South Africa. Julie recruits her rich father's lawyers. They appeal, maybe they'll bribe …

7. The appeal fails. He must return to poverty and despair.

8. Julie declares that she will go too—as his wife!

9. They leave South Africa. At Ibrahim's home village, Julie struggles to make a new life and not be a burden to his big, impoverished family.

10. Ibrahim battles every day to get a visa for another rich country: Canada, or maybe Australia … To stay in this dead-end place will crush him.

11. They nearly lose all respect by having sex during daytime in Ramadan. Ibrahim's mother fears that Julie is corrupting her son.

12. They visit an agricultural scheme, making the desert bloom. Julie wants to invest some of her own SA money in such a scheme, but Ibrahim scorns the idea: 'It's wasted here!'

13. Julie realises that she has come to love Ibrahim's people, possibly more than he does.

14. Ibrahim succeeds in getting them visas to the USA!

15. Preparing for departure: they are leaving this poverty-struck hell-hole for the paradise of the USA.

16. The twist: Julie is not going. Her heart is now here, in this poor country among people that she has grown to love.

17. The separation. Ibrahim heads for America, and Julie is left to ponder.

You should have little difficulty identifying many of the three-act structural points here, such as the catalyst and the inciting incident—and it at once becomes apparent that yes, there *is* a structure. However, you may hesitate: for example, there is clearly a turning point *either* at Step 7 *or* at Step 8—but which? Is it the realisation that Ibrahim must go home, or is it Julie's decision to go with him as his wife?

Where you think that turning point comes will depend on whose story you think this is. If you recall the discussion of the 'character arc' (Chapter Two, p.9), you may consider: which character in this story changes? The answer is pretty clear, even in my condensed version. Ibrahim at the end wants exactly what he wanted at the outset: to live in a rich country. But Julie has changed from a rather shallow young woman to someone who discovers deeper values. *The Pickup* is Julie's story, and the turning point is not Step 7, but Step 8—Julie's decision.

In fact, you will see that most of the key moments of this story consist of decisions: to appeal; to marry; to leave; to invest; to stay. As discussed in Chapter Five: a story is frequently a matter of placing a character in a new situation, and seeing how they react.

Notice two other things here:

Firstly, *The Pickup* is a long way from being a blockbusting Hollywood melodrama. It is a quiet, reflective, intelligent literary novel by a major author. But precisely because it is not an especially dramatic story, it needs the spine that this structure gives it, to keep it moving.

Secondly, the story has a surprising number of things in common with *Casablanca*. Both are set in an Africa dominated by whites, and in both a homeland becomes threatening. Both involve a difficult journey to another land, and a dilemma: whether or not to travel on together? Both involve refugees and permits and borders, and a search for freedom. Both involve a close examination of the central characters' love for each other. Both involve marked changes in life's circumstances. At the end, both are about renunciation. These are some of the great themes of fiction.

The world

It is worth stressing that 'the world' of a story can be anything, but it must be consistent in its rules. For example, in an early short story by Michel Faber—*Fish*—the world is our own and largely recognizable except for one thing: fish can fly.[36] They swim about in the air. Everything in the story follows from this. The people sleep inside tents of fine wire mesh to keep off the nibbling minnows (which can be heard pinging off the mesh all night). And outside during the day one must be constantly aware of the peril of sharks and stingrays. This behaviour of the fish is never explained or gone into; it is simply a premise of the world of the story.

If your world is consistent, your readers will be drawn in and you can do anything. If not, the reader will never quite trust the narrative; tension, characterisation and plotting will all become unconvincing. This is where amateurishness often reveals itself—especially when authors lose their nerve and start making jokes about the world of an otherwise serious story.

The coda

Many novels—and plays, and films—have a coda (Italian for "tail"). The coda may be very short, or it may be a whole chapter, but it provides a moment for the characters to consider the new way the world looks, now that the dust has settled, and for us readers or audience to absorb what we have witnessed.

Here is a Shakespearean coda, the last lines of *King Lear*. The tragedy is overwhelming; the stage is littered with corpses, good and bad; Lear, his daughter and his poor fool are all dead. Things could hardly look worse, and (says the Duke of

---

[36] First published in *Scotland on Sunday* in 1996, and reprinted in the collection *Some Rain Must Fall* (1998).

Albany): 'Our present business is general woe'. But one of the survivors, Edgar, concludes the play with these words:

> The weight of this sad time we must obey;
> Speak what we feel, not what we ought to say.
> The oldest hath borne most; we that are young
> Shall never see so much, nor live so long.

Edgar tells us to face the facts, and to face them honestly (what a modern-seeming sentiment, that second line!) But in Edgar's words there is hope: the mere fact that we can speak about the disaster means that we are not all dead. The tragedy is over, Edgar says. It is a terrible tale but already it belongs to a previous generation, and "we that are young" shall move on. We, the audience, are given a moment to reflect, to calm down, to leave the theatre on our own two feet, shaken but not bowed.

What codas do we find in novels? There may be loose ends to be tied; *Middlemarch* takes a full chapter to do it. Sometimes the main characters pick themselves up and depart from the scene, shaking hands and wishing each other well; sometimes their paths will cross again briefly, and they perhaps recognise each other (J.G. Farrell's *Siege of Krishnapur*) or they don't (Deborah Moggach's *Tulip Fever*). *Madame Bovary* climaxes in Emma's suicide, but thereafter we learn something of what became of her husband Charles and their daughter, and in the very last paragraph (see p.63 above) by a shift of tense we are neatly returned to the present day.

Sophie's Choice, a terrifying novel of the Nazi concentration camps and their aftermath, climaxes in a double suicide. As an ending, this could scarcely be more grim. But there follows another nine pages which the author, William Styron, calls 'A Study in the Conquest of Grief'. These begin with an account (faintly comic) of the funeral, then a meditation on the meaning of Auschwitz, and finally the narrator falling asleep on a beach, awaking to a blue-green sky, consoled as far as possible and thinking: 'This was not judgement day—only morning. Morning: excellent and fair.'

Just so, at the end of *Wuthering Heights*, the narrator Nelly Dean calms us down—we, the stirred and excited readers—as she walks away past the churchyard remarking the graves of the tumultuous trio of lovers: Cathy, Edgar Linton and Heathcliff:

> I lingered round them, under that benign sky; watched the moths fluttering among the heath and harebells; listened to the soft wind breathing through the grass; and wondered how anyone could ever imagine unquiet slumbers for the sleepers in that quiet earth.

Varying narrative structure

Novels (good and bad) may correspond to three-act structure quite loosely, and the type of book you are writing will affect the emphasis you give. With episodic forms like the Bildungsroman or the picaresque, building towards an overall climax is less crucial; the culmination of a picaresque story can be quite perfunctory, because high drama is not what that sort of book is after.

Nonetheless, three-act structure can be found in surprising places. Even that tiny, 49-word story by Robert Louis Stevenson—*The Citizen & The Traveller*—demonstrates this structure also. Go back to it a moment (p.12): there's a world—the market—and a catalyst: the meeting of two strangers. There's an inciting incident, in their beginning a discussion of the market's quality and size. There are steps subtly but, I think, clearly marked in the dialogue, as the traveller becomes more assertive. As in Greek tragedy, there is an offstage climax, the killing of the traveller. And there is a coda: the burial.

But what of more complex or multi-fibred fictions? Do they use the same structure? Frequently, yes—for there is no reason why you cannot have several stories running concurrently, each of them taking the same basic shape. We may be talking about a subplot, subsidiary to the main story, or it may be—as in *Middlemarch*, or William Nicholson's *Secret Intensity of Everyday Life*—that there are several story threads that gradually come together. But each one will have its own structure, its own spine. Many a modern novel appears on the surface to be built up from a mosaic of impressions rather than anything resembling three acts. But these too will often prove, on examination, to have a similar skeleton.

Many tricks and variations can be played: you can, for example, tell the history backwards, as in Martin Amis's *Time's Arrow*. But even here, although we go backwards in time, the structure of the story—the book we read—will likely follow a dramatic course, building its tensions and its turning points.

Editing or developing your structure

A caution: just as it can be tempting to write ever-more-polished prose, so you may think of developing ever-more-complex structures. This can be a particular danger when a story seems not to be working, so that you feel you need more machinery to make clear what is happening, or to add more interest, or to reveal more information …

Usually, this is a mistake. If it is not clear what is going on in your story, then adding another layer of narration, or more flashbacks, or another subplot, or a prologue is unlikely to save it. More literary machinery will make matters more confusing, not less so. It will also make the book seem ever-more-artificial, thus reducing its human impact, not increasing it.

I will suggest (Chapter Sixteen) that the more your prose style draws attention to itself, the less effective it will be. The same goes for structures. The reader should not be thinking about the structure, but should be led through the story. The structure underlying that story will give us confidence that the author knows where we are all heading. If, by contrast, you read of an author suggesting that their novel is structured like a maze or a labyrinth, you should feel suspicious; after all, the purpose of a maze or labyrinth is to confuse those who enter it.

Plenty of fine works of fiction have loose structures which are hardly apparent; Anton Chekhov's great novella *My Life* is an example in which the structure is so delicate as to be scarcely visible.[37] The skill of the novelist is to control structure just enough to *serve* the story, and no more.

---

[37] See Chapter Fifteen for further brief discussion of *My Life*.

Summary points

- Three-act structure: a fundamental technique you should master.
- A quiet, reflective novel needs a structure just as much as does an action adventure.
- Create a world, and keep it consistent.
- Never lose sight of the main question, but build your sequences around subsidiary questions also.
- Make sure that the stakes are raised and the tempo increases as the story proceeds. Pacing is essential.
- Consider using a coda.
- Don't be tempted by ever-more complex structures.

8 **Research: Digging for truffles**

Novelists have always written about other places, other times, and professions other than their own. Chaucer wrote about ancient Troy. Most of George Eliot's novels were set in some earlier period, or in Renaissance Italy. Tolstoy's *War & Peace* concerns a French invasion that occurred half a century before he wrote. When Henry James wrote his essay *The Art of Fiction*, he was in part replying to a critic, Walter Besant, who had urged that one should only write what one knows: 'A young lady brought up in a quiet country village should avoid descriptions of garrison life,' wrote Besant. 'Nonsense', retorted James: use your imagination—and (we might add) do your research.

Many contemporary novels are described as 'superbly researched'—and indeed, research to a certain level has (with the internet, Google and Wikipedia) never been easier; there is a plethora of websites to answer almost any question. Any historical novel, or novel set on the other side of the world, or among practitioners of some arcane science, can be stuffed with detail. Research—whether *primary* (going to the place, interviewing witnesses) or *secondary* (reading about it) can be fun; indeed, research can seem so much more gratifying than writing that one may endlessly put off the real work. Anyone can tap a query into Google. Not everyone can turn the results into fiction.

But what exactly is research for?

You may answer: to make descriptions convincing, and to bring the subject to life. However, the effect can be the opposite. I heard of a man who was completing a novel on which he had been working for decades. It was set in the south of England in the 1920s, and the reason it had taken him so long—the author proudly declared—was that his research had been meticulous to the point of perfection. He had, for instance, obtained railway timetables for those years, so that his fictional trains departed at precisely the times that real trains would have departed at the date in question. This novel was drowning in research.

However, many writers still feel the need to pack their work with detail, some of it over-familiar: a novel about the Second World War hardly seems complete without reference to Standard Eight cars, the difficulties of obtaining nylons, and envy of the neighbour's refrigerator. There will be mention of brands of soap powder, custard powder, and tooth powder. In such novels, characters may not just smoke cigarettes; they must smoke Craven A and Black Cats. They may not own a mere radio; it must be a Bush wireless. Reading such novels is like visiting a museum.

There is a story by Jorge Luis Borges, *On Rigor in Science*, in which the official map-makers of a certain empire determine to make their map of the country 100% accurate. However, to do this, it is clear that the map must also be 100% full-scale—that is, exactly the same size as the empire itself.[38]

Too much researched detail, and you could be heading that way.

The character of the times

In an essay in the *Times Literary Supplement*, the novelist Edmund White pointed out that, "Dickens and George Eliot almost never invoke the products of their day".[39] White argued that the attempt to recreate a period through its material goods is futile, if you get the brand names right but the social conventions, opinions and behaviour wrong.

What matters are the unspoken rules and regulations that epitomise society at a certain time, and its attitudes to (for example) class and sex. White himself was concerned with attitudes toward homosexuality in US society in the

---

[38] The story—118 words long in Spanish—purports to be an extract from a 17th century book of travels. The full text can be seen on various websites, sometimes as *On Exactitude in Science* (in Spanish: *Del rigor en la ciencia*).

[39] "More history, less nature". TLS July 25th, 2003.

1950s. This may be a matter of finely nuanced detail. In Henry James's *The Portrait of A Lady*, the central character Isabel Archer has married Gilbert Osmond, a fastidious art collector living in Italy. In a key passage, Isabel realises that her new husband is continuing an affair—is "intimate"—with an old love called Serena Merle. Isabel realises this when she comes home from an outing to find that Madame Merle is visiting. Before either her husband or the visitor notice her, Isabel glimpses them together through a doorway:

> Madame Merle was standing on the rug, a little way from the fire; Osmond was in a deep chair, leaning back and looking at her. Her head was erect as usual, but her eyes were bent on his. What struck Isabel first was that he was sitting while Madame Merle stood; there was an anomaly in this that arrested her …
>
> 'Didn't he ask you to sit down?' Isabel asked with a smile.

An anomaly: Serena stands, Osmond sits. That is all Isabel needs. Such minutiae of manners and convention will be hard work for a writer from another time to imagine or discover.

Black Cat cigarettes may add a useful dash of period flavour, but getting the behaviour and social attitudes right is far more important. Imagine, for example, a novel which describes a young woman teaching at a British university just before World War Two, struggling to keep her studies and her seminars going while having a baby. This looks like a potentially poignant story—but it would be nonsense, because a woman would not be in that situation in 1939; she would have been sacked, because babies and university employment were seen as incompatible.[40]

I heard someone speak about society balls in London in the 1950s, and how—from the point of view of the nice young men—there were two sorts of girl at such occasions: the sort that one married, and the sort that one slept with. It is distinctions like this which bring period writing alive,

---

[40] This happened to my father's university tutor, Stefanya Ross, wife of linguist Alan Ross.

not details of proprietary bleach, cars and fashions, and it is things like this which need to be correct.

Human passions may change little over time, but in different historical periods they will reveal themselves differently. Violence on the streets, for example, can happen in any town in any epoch—but how is it regarded? Edmund White's *TLS* essay gives the example of street fights in Shakespeare:

> The high aristocratic passion of *Romeo and Juliet* is the destructive, overbred sentiment characteristic of a privileged caste descended from hot-headed warriors but now evolved into a court society with a nostalgia for the violence and cruel caprice of the past. The tragic hopelessness of high passion struck court audiences of the seventeenth century as admirable: noble, proof of the characters' high birth, a form of emotional conspicuous consumption. Those characters were placed in a historical setting in faraway Italy or Greece in order to free the author's fantasy from the restraints of realism.

If we compare *Romeo and Juliet* with its 1957 New York reincarnation *West Side Story*,[41] it is clearly the same tale, but by the 1950s, gang brawls were appropriate not to aristocrats but to the poor side of town. I saw a stage production of *West Side Story* in Edinburgh in 2009 and realised that, although it appeared a faithful recreation of the 1950s original, a change had occurred almost in passing: an 'almost rape' became a rape indeed. Of course, people were raped in the 1950s and in the 1550s; what had changed was what the public considered acceptable on stage.

The novelist must be aware of many things: above all, how society works at the time and place in question. This is what you discover by reading contemporary accounts.

Details do matter—sometimes

I am not saying that details don't matter. Details can have a particular tone or texture that is characteristic of a period or

---

[41] The musical with music by Leonard Bernstein and lyrics by Stephen Sondheim.

a location (do you remember how certain plastics used to have a peculiar acid taste in the mouth if you licked them?). If you get detailing wrong, your reader may be jolted, may object, and may cease to be persuaded by anything you write.

But every novelist makes small errors of fact. A friend told me of his reaction to a work by a leading British novelist, set in Venice; my friend lived in Venice and knew it well. He had spotted two errors that annoyed him. Firstly, someone visits John Ruskin's Venetian home, looks out of a window and is able to see a particular church. My friend objected: he knew Ruskin's house, he had looked out of that window, and he was adamant: the church in question could not be seen. It was just wrong. The second error was that characters went to a nightclub in a basement. A basement—in Venice? Did the author not know that Venice was built on timbers driven into the mud of a lagoon? Had that somehow passed him by? Any basement in Venice would be a stew of silt and rats and the waters of the Adriatic.

These two errors seem to me different in quality: the first is a point of fact, but is unimportant; it does not upset one's broad notion of Venice. The second offends against the very nature of the place. If you know so little about Venice, don't set novels there.

But a full-blooded distortion of reality may be invaluable if it serves the story. In *The Da Vinci Code*, Dan Brown made his villain an albino monk working for the Spanish Catholic fellowship Opus Dei. A spokesman for the real Opus Dei remarked scornfully that, as an entirely lay organisation, they were not big on albino monks. Brown, however, calculated that his readers would find the combination of an albino monk with a secretive religious society uniquely sinister—and (commercially at least) he was right.

Digging for truffles

Forget pedantic accuracy: instead, in your research you should be digging for truffles—those tiny nuggets of intense flavour that bring cooking and writing alive. This is what

Vladimir Nabokov meant when he urged readers to "fondle the details" (Lectures on Literature, 1980). For a story set in Chile, I investigated the Battle of Coronel (November 1914), the first defeat of the Royal Navy since the Napoleonic era. I found many accounts of the tactics, the ships, the order of battle—but one detail stood out: a British naval surgeon observed how many sailors jumping into the sea were wearing a new patented life-saver, an inflatable rubber ring designed to hold the chin out of the water. These men—escaping a horrible death on a burning ship—leaped one by one into the swell, where the inflatable ring whipped their chins back and snapped their necks. This was, in itself, of small significance compared to the overall disaster, but it seemed to encapsulate the tragedy. I can imagine an entire story concerning the surviving doctor returning to London to confront the man who had designed those 'lifesavers'.

Such are the details that a writer instinctively gathers and hoards. In a radio interview, Lorrie Moore discussed her novel *A Gate At The Stairs* and a tiny point of description: a dead squirrel hit by a car, with the little pool of blood coming from its mouth resembling a speech bubble in a cartoon. When the interviewer mentioned this, Moore was delighted:

> I'm very pleased that you noticed that, because I'm very fond of that one, because I did notice this dead squirrel and I thought, that's exactly what it looks like, it looked like it was speaking its blood, and its tail was still moving in the wind.

She remarked that she takes a notebook with her at all times, to record such things.

The important 'finds' in research are often like this: accidental, and visual. They may be found in photographs or exhibitions as often as in texts. I researched extensively for my own novel on 1950s Tibet, *Blue Poppies*; my sources included books of travel, history and anthropology, and *Tintin In Tibet*. But one of the most fertile discoveries was pure chance: I had to visit the dentist, and in his waiting room there was a back copy of *National Geographic* magazine with an article about salt caravans in the Himalayas. I confess: I stole it. At home, I mined the photographs for tiny points of colour and texture, construction and materials, the way a trader builds from his bags and trade goods a temporary shelter against the snow.

A few serendipitous details are more effective than a painstaking reconstruction, and those details should concern not the technicalities of a situation, but the ways in which people experience it. Wanting to write about a 1970s train hijack in the Netherlands, I read any amount of written reports, but my stroke of luck was to meet one of the hostages. He told me something unforgettable: because the hijacked train had stopped on a cambered curve, the trapped passengers had to sit for several days on seats that were at a slope, as a result of which they all became very uncomfortable and then numb in one buttock, and had to keep changing places to turn round. Another eyewitness—a householder I met by chance near the site of the hijacks in northern Holland—told me how his house had formed part of the armed ring surrounding the hostage train, and how when the final assault began, he heard a strange sound: it was young soldiers out in his yard, Catholic boys from the south, who had fallen to their knees and were praying aloud. I would never have learned that from the internet.

Some is dry as dust

Nonetheless, the imagination may be sparked by the driest source. In *The Vessel of Wrath,* W. Somerset Maugham builds his research into the tale. This is the opening of the story:

·There are few books in the world that contain more meat than the *Sailing Directions* published by the Hydrographic Department by order of the Lords Commissioners of the Admiralty … For three shillings you can get Part Three of the *Eastern Archipelago Pilot,* 'comprising the N.E. end of Celebes, Molucca [etc.]' … These business-like books take you on enchanted journeys … It is no common book that offers you casually turning its pages such a paragraph as this: 'Supplies: A few jungle fowl are preserved, the island is also the resort of vast numbers of sea birds. Turtle may be found in the lagoon … A small store of tinned provisions and spirits is kept in a hut for the relief of shipwrecked persons. Good water can be obtained from a well near the landing-place.' Can the imagination want more material than this to go on a journey through time and space?

Research can reveal tempting detail about certain human activities, but beware: although the intricacies of some arcane trade or profession may be intriguing, they do not in themselves make a story. It is the experiences of people that will engage a reader; you will learn nothing of the craft of the Victorian stonemason from Hardy's *Jude The Obscure,* but no one will forget the children hanging dead in the cupboard. One could say little about the 19th century Moscow fashion industry based on a reading of *War & Peace,* but readers remember Pierre Bezukov stumbling around the Battle of Borodino in a tall white hat. On the other hand, where we see what a way of life does to people, it can hardly fail to be interesting—as, for example, in Michel Faber's *The Crimson Petal & The White,* a carefully researched picture of Victorian prostitution in London, and a woman's tactic to survive that experience. Second-rate science fiction often makes the error of thinking the science more interesting than the people, whereas, in a first-rate writer like J.G. Ballard, that is never the case.

There is another approach to research: you could make it all up. The novels of Jim Crace give an impression of painstakingly careful enquiry. In *Being Dead* he describes in gloating detail the processes by which two people murdered among the sand dunes decay and are eaten by bugs and scavengers large and small.

They were far too rotten now and far too rank to hold much allure for gulls and crabs. They'd been passed down, through classes, orders, species, to the last in line, the lumpen multitude, the grubs, the loopers and the millipedes, the button lice, the tubal worms and flets, the *bon viveur* or nectar bugs, which had either too many legs or none. The swag fly maggots had started to emerge on this fourth day from their pod larvae, generated by the putrid heat in Joseph and Celice's innards ….

This has the feel of careful, well-utilised investigation, the author patiently distilling his sources. But sometimes Crace's writing becomes more 'academic':

There was even a specialist cicada in South America (*Entomology,* vol. *CXXI/27*) that fed and bred in diesel engines. It lived on emulsified fuel. Its common name? The grease monkey. It had first been identified in the 1970s in Ecuador. It was wingless, with short legs, designed for clinging, not for mobility ….

In a *Times Literary Supplement* essay on the novels,[42] Edmund Gordon wrote of Crace's "facts":

Crace fabricates everything from landscapes and languages to scientific theories, preferring to invent his material rather than to dilute his imagination with research. His novels abound in counterfeit expertise. He told us all about Victorian shipping and agriculture in *Signals of Distress* (1994), about the hunting techniques of Middle Eastern nomads in *Quarantine* (1997), and about several branches of natural history in *Being Dead* (1999). How much of this knowledge is drawn from the world outside his fiction scarcely matters; it is gospel within it, and to criticize his work for inaccuracy is to underestimate its indifference to the values of realism.

Is there really such a cicada as the "grease monkey"? You would have to do some counter-research to find out. But Crace's imagination is so powerful, his detailing so

---

[42] "Less than turtles: Jim Crace's break with the past". TLS April 16th 2010.

consistent, and—above all—its human significance so well considered, that we believe what he writes *while we read*, never mind that the textbooks might object.

> **WORK POINT:** imagine that you are assisting a Chinese novelist who has never left their native Shanghai, and who is wanting to write a novel set in 1960s Great Britain—in Birmingham, or perhaps Snowdonia. What sources would you recommend to your Chinese author, by way of research? What sort of detail would you pass on to them?

Specialities

Certain sorts of fiction demand a higher level of detail: police procedurals, for example, or scientific thrillers. The information is never hard to find; the Society of Authors even organises trips to Edinburgh police stations, so that crime writers can get it right. Often, a polite letter will earn you permission to visit a particular location and record all the detail that you need. But remember that you will bore your readers silly if you think that you need to pack everything you discover into your work. Again: the details that matter are those that reveal the human experience.

The crucial thing is telling a story, finding the characters, the tension, and the conflict—not the train timetable or the wiring diagram.

Talking proper

If you are writing a period story, an important reason for reading contemporary material is to get a feel for speech. Researching language is important not because you must attempt some quaint reconstruction of (for example) Elizabethan English, but because you will jolt your readers if you write something glaringly anachronistic. It is annoying enough to have Queen Elizabeth snarl at Sir Francis Drake: "Just … do it!" But if your 16th century characters describe the Spanish Armada as "recycled carbon", this might be factually true of wooden ships and indeed sailors but would be absurd, not only because the word 'carbon' was not in use *circa* 1588, but because people in the 16th century did not think of wood (or Spaniards) in quite those terms.[43]

So the point is not merely to get the vocabulary right, but to imagine what people might have talked *about,* and what they thought of it. In all research: the key is not reconstruction but the human experience.

Reconstruction of period speech can be worse than anachronistic vocabulary. Think of those dismally stiff Regency costume dramas in which characters say, "I adore a gavotte, do not you?" The same stuff occurs in period novels. I cannot believe that anyone spoke like that; the contraction "don't" was established in spoken English by 1600, and the absurd period rendition is perhaps based on a misreading of the publishing conventions of the time which did not allow for the contraction in print. It is as bad as having your character say, "I guess a gavotte's a gas!".

Certain novelists have created an entirely new idiom: famously, Anthony Burgess in *A Clockwork Orange.* But this is an invention, not a reconstruction: the novel is set in the future, and Burgess supplies just as much as he needs to create a sense of menace and peculiarity.

It is not only spoken language that you may want to reflect; there is also the written language of, for example, the professions. Ian McEwan's novel *Enduring Love* concerns a character with an obsessive attachment disorder. McEwan gives, as an appendix, a psychiatrist's report, as though lifted from the medical case notes. My wife (a doctor) was so convinced by this that she could hardly believe it was not genuine. "It can't be made up," she told me, "the language, the tone—that's a real doctor writing". As a good professional novelist, McEwan had absorbed the idiom of another profession, presumably by reading a number of such reports or academic articles.

---

[43] 'Carbon' is first recorded in English in 1789.

But however you write speech or imitate the language of the day, if it draws attention to itself to the point where we are noticing the language at the expense of the characters and the drama, then you are harming your story.

WORK POINT: take a speech—pretty much any speech—from a contemporary novel set among people in modern England, and try recasting it as though spoken by Amazonian indians, Ancient Egyptian boatmen or 19th century Australian miners. Try several versions. Which version convinces you most—or least? What do you gain or lose in the attempt?

Summary points

- Too much research detail will kill your novel. Look for quirky, surprising points that add life.
- Accuracy about manners, conventions and attitudes is far more important than brand names and timetables.
- Many errors are unimportant. Errors that matter are those that go against the essence of a place or period.
- Feel free to invent. If you can't find the details you want, make them up. Remember: you are telling a story.
- Avoid anachronisms—but only try to recreate the language or speech of a time or place if you can do it without seeming stiff and pedantic.
- It is more important to know what people would have talked *about*, than to reconstruct period speech.

Landscape, townscape, weather

Landscape and mood

Here is a description of a landscape, part of the extensive moorland of south-west England. The language has been skilfully chosen to create not just a visual effect but also a particular mood. Read it carefully, noting everything that contributes:

> … behind the peaceful and sunlit countryside there rose ever, dark against the evening sky, the long, gloomy curve of the moor, broken by the jagged and sinister hills.
>
> We curved upwards through deep lanes worn by centuries of wheels, high banks on either side, heavy with dripping moss and fleshy hart's-tongue ferns. Bronzing bracken and mottled bramble gleamed in the light of the sinking sun. Still steadily rising, we passed over a narrow granite bridge and skirted a noisy stream which gushed swiftly down, foaming and roaring amid the grey boulders. Both road and stream wound up through a valley dense with scrub oak and fir. At every turn [my companion] gave an exclamation of delight … to his eyes all seemed beautiful, but to me a tinge of melancholy lay upon the countryside … Yellow leaves carpeted the lanes and fluttered down upon us as we passed. The rattle of our wheels died away as we drove through drifts of rotting vegetation …

From the gloomy curve to the dripping moss, the sinking sun, the narrow bridge, the grey stone, the dense woods, the decaying leaves, the coldly metallic "bronzing" bracken … every sentence adds to the effect. This passage comes from an early chapter of *The Hound of The Baskervilles*; after hearing of the ghastly deaths in the Baskerville family, Sherlock Holmes has sent Dr Watson to investigate and to look after Sir Henry Baskerville, who has never before seen his newly-inherited estate (hence his delight). One cannot quite say whether Watson's foreboding is created by the landscape, or whether his impression of the landscape is coloured by his fears; one can certainly say that the effect is deliberate.

Writing a century later, in his spy novel *Restless*, William Boyd does something similar. In the opening pages, a young teacher drives out through the Cotswold countryside to a village, to visit her paranoid mother:

> … the manor house was falling down, on its last woodwormed legs … There was a small damp dark church near by, overwhelmed by massive black-green yews that seemed to drink the light of day; a cheerless pub … The lanes in the village were sunk six feet beneath high banks with rampant hedges growing on either side, as if the traffic of ages past, like a river, had eroded the road into its own mini-valley, deeper and deeper, a foot each decade. The oaks, the beeches, the chestnuts were towering, hoary old ancients, casting the village in a kind of permanent gloaming during the day and in the night providing an atonal symphony of creaks and groans, whispers and sighs as the night breezes shifted the massive branches and the old wood moaned and complained.

The effects here are much like Conan Doyle's, and the intention is the same: by painting the landscape like this, a mood of foreboding is established. And sure enough, when the narrator reaches her mother's house, she finds her mother believing that someone is out to kill her.

As noted in Chapter Seven, early in any fiction you must establish "the world of the story". This is what Conan Doyle and Boyd are both doing; their worlds are alive, and take an active role in the storytelling.

Thomas Hardy was a master of landscape description; he was a fine amateur naturalist, with acute powers of observation. Hardy's *Return of The Native* and also Joseph Conrad's *Nostromo* begin with long landscape descriptions; Hardy's entire first chapter is a description of (fictional) Egdon Heath with not a single human in sight, while Conrad surveys the Bay of Sulaco in a fictional country much resembling Colombia, with reference only to settlers in the distant past. It might be thought that modern readers would want the story to get moving, and would not accept such a leisurely start.[44] But readers are quickly engaged if they *feel* that something is happening, and besides: the story is moving. Conan Doyle, Boyd, Hardy and Conrad are working on our expectations and our apprehensions. Conrad tells us of the rumour of gold in the ground at Sulaco, such that when we look closely at the little town, we know that the hunt for wealth drives the tale. When the first figure appears on Hardy's Egdon Heath, we expect him, as though his shadow had already arrived.

William Boyd's *Restless* also repeats the trick used by Hardy in *Tess of The D'Urbervilles*: both novels begin with a short introduction to the characters of the novel and the conflicts in their lives—and then we get a description of the landscape: the Cotswold village in *Restless*, a Wessex village in *Tess*. Thus, when we look at the scenery, we are already "reading it", looking for the tensions.

> **WORK POINT:** suppose you were re-writing Boyd's *Restless*, beginning with a jolly grandmother driving out to the Cotswolds where she is to re-meet her first true love? How (if at all) might you alter the passage?

Landscape and emotion

A landscape may set the mood; it may also reflect the emotions. In my own first novel *Blue Poppies*, a remote Tibetan village is threatened by the Chinese invasion

---

[44] Extended landscape openings are not so common in 19th century fiction either; only the finest novelists could handle them. Many films, however, begin with a lingering opening shot that establishes a landscape: the protracted leaf fall that begins *Forrest Gump*, or the flight over the rooftops of New York that opens *West Side Story*, or the long aerial look at a city park that begins F.F. Coppola's *The Conversation*, a view into which we are very slowly drawn.

of 1950. The villagers decide that they must flee all together, the beginning of a bitter journey that may lead to exile:

> A short distance from the village, the trail began its diagonal climb up the mountain flank towards the first pass. The throng turned to single file on the narrow track. At the crest of the pass, two miles from the village and several hundred feet higher, the broad saddle was covered with a dusting of snow through which dead yellow grasses stuck. Here, the lead riders paused.
>
> At last, they looked back. Almost everyone they knew was strung along the trail and climbing towards them. As each family reached the summit, they too turned to gaze at the distant village, every detail visible in this thin, clean air. Nothing seemed out of the ordinary, except for the unusual quantity of prayer flags that still hung on every house, across every gate to keep the Chinese out. But scarcely a living soul was visible in the lanes. No children played, there were no dogs, no traders or market wives, no animals, no smoke from fires.
>
> As … the villagers gathered in silence and looked down, a delicate sound reached them in faint wisps and snatches. It was a tiny ringing pain, trembling with unhappiness. A light wind was rising along the river valley, passing through the village towards the pass. As it went amongst the deserted houses, it had found a hundred little prayer bells on cords and on springs in courtyards, windows and doorways. Touched and shaken, the shivering of these bells reached the people in the pass.

Here, several things emphasise the poignancy of the situation: there is the high pass, the point of no return, and the longing look back at their homes; and there is a sound, that "tiny ringing pain" that comes to them on the wind from the village. It is, of course, not actually the bells that are feeling miserable.

A distant view can be exhilarating and thrilling too. At the start of Thomas Hardy's *Jude the Obscure*, Jude is a penniless country boy who dreams of becoming a great scholar at "Christminster". He decides that he wants a look at that marvellous city, which is some way from where he lives. Again, the choice of language is very deliberate, emphasising the sacred regard Jude has for scholarly learning. The view is described in Biblical tones: Jude ascends the ladder praying for a revelation, which comes in the guise of precious stones—as in the vision of St John.[45] Here is the Bible:

> He shewed me that great city, the holy Jerusalem, descending out of heaven from God, having the glory of God, and her light was like unto a stone most precious, even like a jasper stone, clear as crystal.

And here is young Jude's first revelation of Christminster:

> It was waning towards evening; there was still a faint mist, but it had cleared a little … He ascended the ladder to have one more look … Perhaps if he prayed, the wish to see Christminster might be forwarded ….
>
> About a quarter of an hour before the time of sunset the westward clouds parted, the sun's … beams streaming out in visible lines between two bars of slaty cloud. The boy immediately looked back in the old direction.
>
> Some way within the limits of the stretch of landscape, points of light like topaz gleamed. The air increased in transparency with the lapse of minutes, till the topaz points showed themselves to be the vanes, windows, wet roof slates, and other shining spots on the spires, domes, freestone-work and varied outlines that were faintly revealed. It was Christminster.

---

[45] Authorised Version, the Revelation of St John the Divine, ch. 21: v. 10–27. Many other precious stones are included in this passage, and their sacred qualities were discussed in medieval texts knows as 'lapidaries'.

Landscape as situation and symbol

We've seen that telling a story may consist of placing a character in a new situation and watching how they react. A landscape, especially a harsh one, can be a situation in itself. Remember that your story needs to be set in a clearly specified world. The same story could be set in other worlds, but the effect would be different. My novel *Blue Poppies*, for instance, concerns a young Scottish radio operator caught up in that Tibetan village's flight from the Chinese invasion, and in the process learning the difference between selfish love and generous loyalty, and the meaning of exile. Thus far, the story could have been set in many different landscapes: the villagers could have been fleeing from inter-galactic storm-troopers, or they could have been retreating through the Amazonian rainforest. Similar lessons might have been learned, and similar characters involved.

But the landscape affects the story deeply. In *Blue Poppies*, humanity is set against an immense Himalayan landscape that makes the people seem both very small, and very exposed and vulnerable. Pushing through a tract of jungle would have a quite different import: there would be claustrophobia, a fear of never knowing who is behind the next tree, of never being sure which way you are travelling because you cannot see the sun … A mood, in fact, of panic and betrayal. The Himalayan setting emphasises the villagers' unimportance in the great scheme of things, but also focuses our attention on them and their moral dilemmas very sharply, because there is no one else for miles around. Placing people out in a wide landscape both isolates them and traps them in the magnifying lens of our attention.

Thus, landscape often has moral properties. The title of a famous WW2 memoir claims that *The Jungle Is Neutral*[46]— but often in fiction it is not. In Jane Austen's *Mansfield Park*, the timid, sickly but sensitive heroine Fanny Price grows

---

[46] By F. Spencer Chapman (1949), describing the war against the Japanese in Malaya. The point of the title is that the jungle is equally harsh on both sides.

increasingly perturbed by the manner in which, left to their own devices, a group of young people are edging towards the limits of decent behaviour. On a visit to a neighbouring and very old great house, there is an embarrassed debate in which Fanny defends old-fashioned standards of piety against modern carelessness; meanwhile, the young group eagerly discuss "improvements" to the venerable grounds such as chopping down an avenue of ancient oaks. Then, Fanny witnesses two of the group—one of whom is engaged to be married elsewhere—forcing their way past a locked gate out of the orderly environs of the house into the untamed landscape beyond. Fanny, sensing the moral wrong that is developing, will not follow their move from order to disorder. Thus, how people behave in a landscape reflects the morals of their society.

Other "big" scenery has symbolic force: the sea is where epic struggles—physical and moral—are played out by personalities set in stark relief, far from any friendly shore: think of Melville's *Moby-Dick*, or Conrad's *Typhoon*, or Hemingway's *The Old Man And The Sea*, or William Golding's *Rites of Passage*. At sea, we learn what people are made of. On dry land, we have for example the boundless Australian desert of Patrick White's *Voss*, and James Vance Marshall's *Walkabout* with two children lost in the outback.

Groups in a landscape

There is in fiction an interesting tradition of the picnic. By taking characters out of their normal context and setting them in a group out in the open, we see their interactions in starker relief. Another Australian example is Joan Lindsay's *Picnic At Hanging Rock*: on Valentine's Day 1900, a party of schoolgirls from a posh boarding school are possessed by some nameless force in the landscape—and disappear. In Jane Austen's *Emma*, it is at a picnic that Emma betrays herself with a cruel jibe. E.M. Forster's *A Passage To India* hinges on a grand picnic at the Malabar caves, in the course of which all sorts of irreconcilable personal and cultural differences between the imperial British and their Indian 'subjects' come to the fore, while there is a sorry irony in the efforts of young Dr Aziz to impose, at the picnic, his sense of the dignity of age-old Indian culture on a landscape that gets the better of him. At the end of the novel, it is the horses and the very rocks of the landscape that announce that reconciliation is a way off as yet.

The South African J.M. Coetzee uses a truly ghastly picnic in his semi-autobiographical novel *Summertime* to show his central character as desperately gauche, socially inept and distracted, but also with a certain dogged conviction. "Mr Coetzee" has invited a Brazilian family he is attempting to befriend to a picnic out of town. The miserable outing is described by the Brazilian mother:

> He did not fetch us in a car, he did not have a car, no, he came in a truck … So the girls in their nice clothes had to sit in the back with the firewood while I sat in the front with him and his father … We drove up into the mountains—we had to stop to let the girls put on their coats, they were getting cold—to a park … a nice place, almost empty now because it was winter. As soon as we chose our place, Mr Coetzee made himself busy unloading the truck and building a fire … And then, even before the fire was burning properly, clouds came over and it grew dark and started to rain. 'It is just a shower, it will soon pass,' said Mr Coetzee … But of course it did not, it went on raining and gradually the girls lost their good spirits. 'Why does it have to rain today of all days?' whined Maria Regina, just like a baby. 'Because it is winter,' I told her, 'because it is winter and intelligent people, people with their feet on the ground, don't go out on picnics in the middle of winter.'
>
> The fire that Mr Coetzee and Joana had built went out.

Human resonances

My wife and I were driving across California. It grew late, and we had a small tent with us, so we turned off up a dirt side-road, driving into wild rising country empty of all humanity. We finally stopped somewhere quite deserted and settled down for the night—only to realise at dawn that we had camped in the middle of what appeared to be an old rural cemetery, surrounded by decaying wooden crosses, small heaps of stone and low mounds in the ground. We left rather promptly.

Landscapes are seldom entirely "natural", but have a human history: of settlement and farming, of battles, of forest clearance, of hunting and trade and travel. You can make use of this. In *The Hound of The Baskervilles*, Conan Doyle repeatedly refers to the primitive huts of ancient people who once dwelt on the bleak moor; we sense a pitiless struggle, ancient and dimly understood lives, humanity grappling with greater forces … all part of the mood of the Sherlock Holmes story.

Landscapes carry a social force. Think of lakes: in the Scottish Highlands, the loch will be the property of the Duke of Something, or of a billionaire foreign investor—certainly not of the men and women who live nearby. However, while you can walk around the margins of almost any Scottish loch, you can't do that round the Italian lakes, because they are ringed with luxury mansions, the shore portioned up and fenced off. If you find yourself by the shores of Lake Michigan, don't fall in; the pollution is frightening (as someone[47] said: in the Great Lakes, you don't drown—you dissolve). And if the lake is high in the Himalayas, there may be no one in sight, but be careful nonetheless; China is to your north, India to your south—and you are walking in a political (perhaps a real) minefield. There is no such thing as a neutral landscape; it will be charged with human tension. Sense it, and use it.

Be aware also of the changes in the countryside. When I moved to rural Scotland, three farms surrounded our village, farms which embodied hundreds of years of history, employing local people and setting the pattern of village life. In our first ten years, all three were sold, and their land absorbed by larger farms further away. All three of our

---

[47] I believe it was John F. Kennedy

local farmhouses became ex-farmhouses. The landscape is peaceful and beautiful—but it is far from static or quiet in a human sense, and it is full of risk: crops fail, subsidies are withdrawn, banks demand repayment, and gruesome accidents happen, particularly to farm children.

Finally, any evocation of landscape will be more acute if you are aware of time: the turn of seasons, the farm year, the incessant change from one human activity to the next. Look at any country scene, and you can be sure it will be different next week.

> **WORK POINT:** look at the landscape nearest your home. How has it changed in the last decade? What social tensions does it reflect? Where is the story in that?

Scents and sounds

Remember that scenery is not only a visual thing; landscapes have smells: the sulphur of volcanic pools; the sweet smells of harvest; hints of oil or rubber smoke in an industrial zone; the salt-and-iodine reek of a seashore. There will also be characteristic sounds; if you are visiting a location, try standing very still with your eyes closed, and registering all the sounds that you can hear. Some of these will be things that you cannot see: machinery in a mine behind a spur of mountain; a motorway just out of sight. Others will be close: what sound do your feet make on the ground beneath you? What are the qualities of the soil or the vegetation, that it makes that sound? A character whose nerves are on edge may be intensely aware of such things.

This is one of the advantages of going to your location, and of carrying a notebook. But once again: never forget that you are telling a story, and creating the world of that story. The features to highlight in the landscape are those that set up the mood of the tale, or prefigure events, or affect the action in a practical sense, or have some other resonance. Think of landscape description not as an "add-on" but as a dynamic part of your storytelling. Think of the human experience of the landscape—just as with any other detail that you extract from your research. Are you describing the iodine stink of the seashore? In 2009 a man walking on the shore in France was killed by gases given off by decomposing seaweed …

I have lately visited two battlefields. The first was Culloden, scene of the last pitched battle fought on British soil (1746) and the end of the romantic "old" Scotland. There are libraries of literature on this battle, all describing the desperate charge of the Highland clans across the heather towards the Hanoverian muskets. But it was only when I walked out onto the open moor that I realised that the heather was deep, dense and springy—and that even walking over it was tricky. The heather was anything but neutral; it sapped the energy out of the Highlanders' charge.

The second location was Breitenfeld, a few miles outside Leipzig in eastern Germany. Here, in 1631, a Protestant Swedish army slaughtered a Catholic Imperial army, and won the first victory for the new religion—a turning point in the Thirty Years War. The battlefield (now bisected by an autobahn and a main-line railway) is a low ridge in open country. Around the margins of the fields, hedges of wild plum trees grow. When I walked there, the over-ripe plums were falling in their thousands and breaking open on the ground; the smashed, split flesh was a deep purple.

The landscape was giving me an echo of the human experience.

Townscapes

I am so familiar with street life and scenery that I often take my knowledge of it for granted. How lazy I sometimes allow my powers of observation to become!

WORK POINT: think of a street location that you know, and write a detailed description of it. Bring the focus close. The shop where you buy milk most mornings: what colour is the front door? Go to the location: were you right? What did you get wrong, and what did you miss?

Observing a cityscape will suggest many small points that can operate in your fiction; in Britain, for example, you may be startled to realise how many CCTV cameras there are (at my tiny local railway station I've counted nineteen). In a tranquil park, there will nonetheless be a fountain or music that drowns out sound, conveniently shielding a furtive conversation from eavesdroppers.[48] There will be smells, not just of traffic: bakers' smells, and coffee, and the scent of warm detergent coming from the door of the launderette, and rotting pizza and urine from the nearby alley. In towns there is always a conflict between the smart and the filthy, as well as surprising juxtapositions of textures—as in the novel *Minaret* by the Sudanese novelist Leila Abouleila whose description of women praying in their long, colourful robes includes, "the fall of polyester on the grass". Often there will be no grass in sight—and some of your characters will loathe the lack of anything natural, while others revel in the entirely man-made environment, just as some people love the realisation that, in their cars, everything is synthetic.

Look always for the human details that will work for you. Describing the drab exterior of a bingo hall is unlikely to have much impact; far more effective to note the radiant heaters fixed to the wall by the outer doors, and the women in leather coats who leave the game and step outside for a cigarette, clustered there.

Cultivate an ear for the sound-scape. Cities are not uniformly noisy; turning a corner may dramatically affect the acoustic properties—which can in turn either relax or shock the visitor. Music is a feature of townscapes (but rarely of the open country), whether it be buskers or musak or the radio playing high upon scaffolding where builders are at work, or the sudden physical thumping through the open window of a boom-box car. Are these things a matter of pleasure or distress to your character? Is this something they love about city life? At the end of *Sophie's Choice*, just before the final tragedy, another character walks the Brooklyn streets and

---

[48] As used brilliantly in the opening of Coppola's 1974 film *The Conversation*.

hears loud classical music pouring from Sophie's bedroom window several hundred yards away. Then it stops …

Townscapes are as redolent of social distinctions and tensions as rural landscapes, and not just in the division into poor or affluent neighbourhoods. It is the incongruities and the changes that make the point: the high streets where the butcher and the deli have closed and the charity shop and betting shop have moved into their place. Look at the newcomers who do not fit in: Hardy's country stonemason Jude, when he first arrives in Christminster, wanders the quadrangles of the ancient colleges by night when there is no one present, but cannot enter the lecture halls by day. In *My Son's Story*, the South African novelist Nadine Gordimer portrays the lives of an educated Coloured family just before the end of Apartheid. She describes Saturdays in their town near Johannesburg, with the family passing the public library that they cannot enter, the tables at which they cannot eat their fish and chips, the toilets in the department store that they cannot use. There is a smell here that is more-than-realistic:

> If—as always—the children needed to go to the lavatory, the parents trotted them off down to the railway station, where there were the only toilets provided for their kind … As some lordly wild animal marks the boundaries of his hunting and mating ground which no other may cross, it was as if the municipality left some warning odour, a scent of unnameable authority, where the Saturday people were not to transgress. And they read the scent always; it had always been there.

In another South African novel, *Summertime*, John Coetzee makes his own small stand by refusing to accept the normal divisions of labour—manual work being for blacks—and insists on making a concrete patio around his suburban house with his own hands. It is almost a disaster: he miscalculates the amounts of concrete required and it takes him far longer than he supposed, shoving barrow-loads by himself. As we gather the physical feel and look of the neighbourhood, we learn its human significance also, and the character of the protagonist: naïve, barely competent, but stubborn in his convictions. We even learn the political resonance of DIY.

> **WORK POINT:** in your own town, what social distinctions can be observed on the street? Who lives where—and are those frontiers moving? Are there streets—even in a small town—that have shopping only for the elite, and which are avoided by poorer people? Who travels on the buses: rich, poor, everyone or no one? Are there cafes for some, and up-market coffee for others? What sort of character might seem most out of place: someone of a certain ethnic grouping—or a struggling farmer in shabby tweeds?
>
> Write a sketch of someone coming to your town for the first time. In what ways might they find this townscape seductive or threatening?

Some writers make particular environments into characters in their story: a modern urban example looms over Catherine O'Flynn's novel *What Was Lost*, a creepy tragi-comedy of a lonely little girl who imagines herself to be a private detective working in a town dominated by a vast shopping mall called Green Oaks. The mall presides over the story like a grim monster. O'Flynn focuses on humble members of staff at Green Oaks: there is Lisa, the "Duty Manager" (long grinding hours of overtime are her duty) of a record store, and Kurt and Gary the security men. Green Oaks comes to control their lives, while taking on a sinister being of its own:

> At times Gary talked about Green Oaks as if it were alive. As if somehow the steel, the glass, the concrete and the people combined to make something bigger, something almost worthy of reverence. Gary had copies of the original plans, he had photographs mapping the centre's changes, rebrands and refits. He was intent on mounting a display of all these in the atrium in the very near future. Did Kurt know why? No he did not, because not many people realized that October 2004 would mark Green Oaks' 21st birthday.

Not many people seemed to think it worth marking. Not many people knew all its secrets.

From the eccentricities of the waste disposal system to the vastness of the car parks; from the grandeur of the public spaces to the meanness of the staff toilets; from the "lift-shitter" they never catch, to the little ghostly girl they glimpse but cannot find; Green Oaks and its ghosts outwits its occupants at every turn. As a setting for a story, it is vividly realised—and has a dynamic presence.

If you are writing about a city in history, or an imaginary city, then you will have to work harder. Imagine that you are led through those streets by someone wishing to show you everything. A good exercise is simply to go for a walk through a town and examine the details, particularly the upper storeys of buildings that one normally does not notice above the shops. Here is Michel Faber in *The Crimson Petal & The White* describing the slums of Victorian London:

> Church Lane is the sort of street where even the cats are thin and hollow-eyed for want of meat … A model lodging-house for the deserving poor, opened with great philanthropic fanfare twenty years ago, has already fallen into the hands of disreputables, and has aged terribly. The other, more antiquated houses, despite being two or even three storeys high, exude a subterranean atmosphere, as if they have been exc-avated from a great pit, the decomposing archaeology of a lost civilisation. Centuries-old buildings support themselves on crutches or iron piping, their wounds and infirmities poulticed with stucco, slung with clothes lines, patched up with rotting wood. The roofs are a crazy jumble, the upper windows cracked and black as the brickwork … However, since you've arrived at ten to three in the middle of a freezing November night, you're not inclined to admire the view.

Everything here has a human reference, even the buil-dings themselves with their "wounds". Writing like this is both a pleasure to read and also great fun to do.

Snow, hail, fog, heat

The American pulp-fiction author Elmore Leonard—a stern advocate of plain writing—published in 2007 his *Ten Rules of Writing*, for the benefit of novelists. His Rule Number One is: never start a book by describing the weather. Readers (says Leonard) will soon be bored; they'll want people, and action; they won't be prepared to wait. This advice echoes the concern about opening a novel with a landscape. But if weather is regarded as a situation that will demand a human reaction, then that can be a powerful opening. In her radio interview about her novel *A Gate At The Stairs*, Lorrie Moore remarked: 'I did feel that I was setting up a kind of ominousness on the first page, that there's something amiss with the weather ... The weather is off.'

Many novels make use of snow: there is *Miss Smilla's Feeling for Snow*, and *Snow Falling on Cedars* ...[49] Snow takes over, dominating the environment and the lives of people. In his *Snow*, Orhan Pamuk sets the story in a town completely snow-bound. It is a tale of deadly political bigotry and of people trapped together by blizzards, people with a (literally) narrow world view. At the end, the snow melts, and at last the narrator can leave; he breathes freely, and sees renewed and broad horizons.

Choke Chain, by another South African, Jason Donald, begins with a hail storm:

> Tiny ball bearings of ice stung my calves and neck as I dashed forward. Seconds later it was like running on marbles. Pain jolted up my legs every time my bare heels landed on a solid ball of ice. Little ice pellets jammed between my toes ... They were now the size of apricots crashing onto my head and shoulders. The force of it bent me double and I stumbled, almost tripping over. Through the deluge I could see Mom waiting by the front door, arms folded tightly across her chest.

---

[49] By Peter Hoeg (1992), and David Guterson (1996).

'Quickly! Quickly, get inside!' …
'I'll get some towels,' I shouted.
Mom grabbed the back of my shirt and pulled me to
the ground.
'No! Stay with me!'

The sitting room window suddenly exploded. The curtains reached in toward us as a freezing gust of air blew in through the burglar bars. Among the shards of glass on the carpet lay a chunk of ice the size of my fist. Another window smashed in the kitchen. Kevin clung to Mom's neck. From down the passage I heard glass shatter in the bathroom. Mom grabbed my wrist and pulled me to the floor. Together we crawled to the centre of the living room and huddled together behind the coffee table while our home disintegrated around us.

The hail storm has three functions: it creates immediate tension; it symbolises the coming disintegration of this family; and through people's reactions to the hail, it begins the process of delineating character and relationships in the household. The hail is experienced through human sensations: the pain, the feeling of ice between the toes, and the menacing way that 'the curtains reached in towards us.'

Fog has a particular quality of threat, like tangible darkness. It can be claustrophobic—as in Elizabeth Bowen's novels of 1940s and 50s London such as *The Death of The Heart*, featuring the infamous smogs—or it can be simply sinister. Guy de Maupassant wrote a whole story (*On The Water*) about a man's fear of fog. The man takes a rowing boat out on the Seine near Paris. In the early evening he stops for a smoke, and drops anchor—but then cannot pull in the anchor and move on; it is stuck. The fog comes over the water:

The river had slowly become enveloped in a thick white fog which lay close to the water, so that when I stood up I could see neither the river, nor my feet, nor the boat … I was as if buried to the waist in a cloud of cotton of singular whiteness, and all sorts of strange fancies came into my mind. I thought that someone was trying to climb into my boat ... and that the river, hidden by the thick fog, was full of strange creatures which were swimming all around me. I felt horribly uncomfortable, my forehead felt as if it had a tight band round it, my heart beat so that it almost suffocated me and, almost beside myself, I thought of swimming away from the place. But then, again, the very idea made me tremble ...[50]

He passes a most unpleasant night. In the morning, someone helps him pull in the anchor—and they drag up the corpse of an old woman with a large stone tied about her neck.

Fog creeps silently. In the denouement of *The Hound of The Baskervilles*, Sherlock Holmes has laid a trap—but all his plans are thrown into deadly disarray by a fog advancing across the moor, preventing Holmes from seeing the murderer he knows to be stalking a new victim:

The night was clear and fine above us [but] every minute, that white woolly plain which covered one half of the moor was drifting closer and closer to the house. Already the first thin wisps of it were curling across the golden square of the lighted window ... As we watched it the fog-wreaths came crawling round both corners of the house and rolled slowly into one dense bank, on which the upper floor and the roof floated like a strange ship upon a shadowy sea.

Heat is just as useful as chill: heat with its effect on people, their short tempers, their sapped energy. Certain novels are pervaded by summer heat, such as *Sophie's Choice*, in which the warmth and the heightened sexuality of summer in Brooklyn in 1947 are cruelly at odds with the torments in Sophie's mind. As the tale reaches its tragic climax, thunder is building ominously, filling the narrator with dread ...

As ever, it is the weather's dynamic effect on people that earns it a place in fiction.

---

[50] Trans. L. Quesada, London, c. 1895.

Summary points

- Landscape description can establish not just a setting but a mood of anticipation.
- Instead of reporting your characters' emotional state, try finding an equivalent aspect of the landscape that may suggest it.
- Different landscapes, such as sea, or desert, or jungle, may have different symbolic or moral force.
- Placing a group of characters out in a wide landscape (as at a picnic, or at sea) isolates them and focuses attention on the group dynamic.
- Almost every landscape has a human history and echo. Use it.
- Townscapes are full of incongruities. Search also for the sounds and the smells, and the human resonances in the buildings.
- Use weather in similar dynamic ways, to increase the momentum of your story, or to isolate groups of people.

10 Interior design

Interiors—those quintessentially man-made environments. Remember that every story is set in a particular world; what could be more powerful than the worlds that people construct to make a certain impression on the rest of us? Here is the home of Jay Gatsby, that quietly polished and impeccably mannered American millionaire, and here are his party guests awed by his faultless style:

> The bar, where we glanced first, was crowded, but Gatsby was not there … On a chance we tried an important-looking door, and walked into a high Gothic library, panelled with carved English Oak, and probably transported complete from some ruin overseas.
>
> A stout, middle-aged man, with enormous owl-eyed spectacles, was sitting somewhat drunk on the edge of a great table staring with unsteady concentration at the shelves of books …
>
> 'What do you think?' he demanded impetuously.
>
> 'About what?'
>
> He waved his hand towards the book-shelves.
>
> 'About that. As a matter of fact you needn't bother to ascertain. I ascertained. They're real.'
>
> 'The books?'
>
> He nodded.
>
> 'Absolutely real—have pages and everything. I thought they'd be a nice durable cardboard …'
>
> He rushed to the book-cases and returned with Volume One of *The Stoddard Lectures*.
>
> 'See!' he cried triumphantly. 'It's a bona-fide piece of printed matter. It fooled me … It's a triumph.

What thoroughness! What realism! Knew when to stop, too—didn't cut the pages.' [51]

Jay Gatsby is in fact not at all the paragon of calm dignity and financial stability that he appears: in reality he's a bootlegger of illicit alcohol with shady business partners. But how could one doubt a man with a library like that—a man, what's more, who doesn't vulgarly pretend to have read the books?

Here is another environment, and its inhabitant:

> On one of the shelves of an old dresser, in company with chipped sauce-boats, pewter jugs, cheese-graters, and paid bills, rested an old and ragged Bible, on whose front page was the record, in faded ink, of a baptism dated ninety-four years ago. 'Martha Crale' was the name written on that yellow page. The yellow, wrinkled old dame who hobbled and muttered about the kitchen looking like a dead autumn leaf which the winter winds still pushed hither and thither, had once been Martha Crale; for seventy-odd years she had been Martha Mountjoy. For longer than anyone could remember she had pattered to and fro between oven and wash-house and dairy, and out to chicken run and garden, grumbling and muttering and scolding, but working unceasingly ... . She was so old and so much a part of the place, it was difficult to think of her exactly as a living thing.[52]

These two proprietors, Gatsby and Martha, are as one with their worlds. But interiors can get to people. Those who work in badly designed offices or hospitals sometimes speak of "sick building disease", a combination of eye-straining light from flickering tubes, poorly filtered air, microbes in the tap water, inadequate sound-proofing, low ceilings ... In Catherine O'Flynn's *What Was Lost*, most of the story is played out in the shopping mall, Green Oaks,

---

[51] F. Scott Fitzgerald, *The Great Gatsby* (1925).
[52] Saki (Hector Hugh Munro) *The Cobweb*—a story in the collection *Beasts & Superbeasts* (1914).

whose interior is having a bad effect on Lisa, one of the staff:

> Lisa sat in the window of Burger King consuming saturated fat and a large carton of sugar. It was a treat … There was something in the air of Green Oaks that made everyone crave the complex non-flavours of highly-processed, industrially honed calorific content—and Lisa was too tired to fight it today … She watched the tail end of the January sales rush stream by on the other side of the glass. There were no windows at Green Oaks and so it was only by looking at the shoppers that you could get some idea of the weather outside. Today everyone was dressed as American footballers …

But this grim experience of the interior is not shared by everyone. Lisa's colleague Kurt is a security guard at Green Oaks. With a failed marriage still hurting, Kurt finds wandering the concrete underbelly of the mall oddly therapeutic:

> Kurt was slowly patrolling through the parallel unseen universe of the service corridors. Mile upon mile of pipes, wires, ventilator shafts, fuse cupboards, security barriers, fire hoses. Like an illuminated cave network, narrow passages would suddenly bloom into cavernous loading bays and other lanes would lead nowhere. Everything glowed grey, everything smelled of hot dust. He would wander for hours in a trance, following no particular route, going through the motions of checking every door handle. Sometimes he would stop and try and sense where he was in relation to the centre, but he rarely came close. He liked to be lost, tangled somewhere in the knotted orbit of the mall.

Once again, this is dynamic description: the human reaction to a situation. In writing fiction, you are always looking for the stresses and conflicts in people's lives, and you find these in the worlds they inhabit.

Of course, many interiors will be hard and cold and devoid of organic life: the empty warehouse, the concrete bunker, the unsold newly-built house. Nonetheless, it is the human echo—even the human absence—that makes the place what it is. It may be the lack of life in a home that sets you thinking: in Nicolas Freeling's *Gun Before Butter*, it is the curious absence of personal touches in a murdered man's Amsterdam flat that starts Inspector Van der Valk's speculations. Similarly, one might visit a family home decorated in pristine white, beautifully tidy, with a mother arraying her three offspring in a mute row upon a white sofa, all in sparklingly clean clothes—and the novelist in you would think: what is wrong with these people? What is amiss in their lives? How might this change?

> **WORK POINT:** imagine that you are visiting a new acquaintance's home. You go to the bathroom: describe its character, and how that reflects your friend's personality. Then imagine returning one year later. Something has changed—something small, but significant. It has you worried. What is it?

To consider the use of interiors, look at a painting: *The Awakening Conscience* (1853)[53] by the Pre-Raphaelite William Holman Hunt shows a smart Victorian man with a woman who has been sitting on his knee but who now rises up. They are surrounded by stuff, all of it new stuff: new furniture, new carpets, a new piano; it is claustrophobically, expensively new. That is because she is the man's mistress, and this is not his house or hers exactly, but a bijou little home in which he has installed her, to be visited for his pleasure. What is uncomfortable about the interior is nothing intrinsic (what's wrong with polished pianos?): it is the situation it reflects. Now the details in the scene take on significance. Some—like the gentleman's hat and gloves dropped casually

---

[53] The painting is in the Tate Gallery, London, and can readily be seen on various websites including Tate Online.

on the table (because he is only visiting)—are part of the narrative. Others—like the cat playing with a wounded bird under the table—are symbolic. A fiction writer might bring a newcomer into this space, have them observe such details, and reach any number of conclusions about the inhabitants of the house even before meeting them. Now, look at a modern interior, a home or an office or whatever; try reading it in this way.

An interior may even be ironic. While on a BBC training course, I was taken to visit the set of the hospital series *Casualty*. There, apparently, was a hospital A&E department, all white walls and equipment and bodies on trolleys, and doctors and nurses in green and white uniforms fussing about the patients. And yet, had I suffered a heart attack just then, nobody would have known what to do. Now, there's a story …

Sensory information

This television stage was instructive in another way: what was missing? The smells of a hospital—disinfectants, vomit, dirty clothes, clean laundry—were absent. So were the sounds. The actors spoke their lines, but most of the sounds—suction machines, rumbling trolleys, beeping monitors—would be added later. This interior without sound or smell seemed creepily unreal; so it would in fiction.

WORK POINT: plan a visit to an interior location—a supermarket, a block of offices. Before going, try to imagine as much as possible of the sensory information that you might encounter. Then make the visit in person. Stay there as long as possible (but avoid being arrested for loitering). Notice the sounds, smells, temperature differences in different areas, colours, and every other impression.

In itself, the colour of a floor is of no importance, but for your story it could be, part of an ambience that leaves a particular character feeling out of place, or that provokes tell-tale reactions: your visitor may be a terrible snob, and may consider the colour scheme awfully vulgar. It may be garishly bright, adding to an already overwrought headache. It may be soft and soundless—with any number of plot implications. It may be hard and loud, like fake wood laminate.

> **WORK POINT:** try lying on the floor. Imagine that you are a hostage, tied up so that you cannot move (so stop trying to get comfortable). Firstly, feel the pressure points on your body. Where do you start to feel sore or numb? Next, without moving your head at all (only your eyes): what can you see? What can you *not* see—the door, perhaps? What can you hear, apart from your own heart and breathing? What tiny sounds are you aware of?

If you try this exercise, consider how the smallest details may contribute to your story. For example, as this trussed-up hostage, you will be alert for any new danger: did you feel a slight cold current of air on your face or your back? Where was that coming from? Might it indicate a door opening? If you hear a gentle ticking sound, is that a bomb timer or just the heating coming on? This tells you that time is passing—or perhaps that visitors are expected. Can you smell food cooking? Is there someone whose attention you might attract, to release you? But how? You perhaps run all these possibilities through your mind, only to conclude that the situation is hopeless—and so despair …

The palimpsest and the museum

Most buildings have a history, often unexpected. I was once commissioned to write a film script concerning an Italian terrorist hiding in the attics of a huge old building. The building in question is quite genuine; it occupies an entire island all to itself, in the lagoon near Venice. It is now a luxurious hotel with a website that tells of its former career as a monastery. What the website does not mention is that over the centuries the island has also been a leper hospital, a plague quarantine and a gunpowder store, and was for more than a century until the early 1980s a mental asylum. For some years (when I visited to research) the only inhabitants were several hundred cats, one of which vomitted on my companion's shoe.

A building like this can be called a palimpsest—that is, a document that has been written over several times, so that there are different historical layers of meaning. If you've ever stripped walls prior to decorating, and found yourself removing older and older layers of patterned paper, you'll know the sensation of going back through time. But what of other alterations: doors that have been moved, colours changed, rooms with new functions? There are a number of stories concerning a young wife's lover bricked into an alcove by a jealous older spouse.[54] Neighbours of mine in Scotland began renovating their cottage and found a room hidden behind the staircase.

Certain people turn a building into a repository of their own history. Think of Charles Dickens' Miss Havisham who was jilted on the day of her wedding: decades later, she sits in her bridal gown surrounded by everything as it was on the wedding day and with the cake still waiting, uneaten except by mice. In Istanbul, Kemal makes a monument to his love by stealing the contents of his beloved's home, teaspoon by teaspoon, over the course of eight years to create his *Museum of Innocence* in her memory, including 4,213 of her cigarette stubs.

Gregorius, the protagonist of *Night Train To Lisbon*, is searching out the story of a long-dead Portuguese author, who had been a doctor and a writer. Gregorius tracks down this man's sister, still living in the home she once shared with

---

[54] The 'walled-in youth' theme is remarkably widespread: examples range from Walerian Borowczyk's film *Blanche* (1971), set in a 12th century castle and based on a 19th century Polish epic, to an infamous modern French horror novel called *Les Emmurrés* ("the walled-in") by Serge Brussolo (2006). There is reputedly a walled-in young nun at Lindisfarne Abbey, Northumberland, and even rock music: Pink Floyd's *The Wall* (1979).

her brother in Lisbon. The brother's study is a shrine, kept exactly as he left it at his death three decades beforehand; the writing chair has not been moved an inch; the same pile of books and papers stands on the floor. The visitor wonders if the coffee grounds in the cup are thirty years old also, and decides that they are. There is just one anomaly: there is no dust anywhere. The sister comes to this shrine every day and dusts it, as though there might be patients arriving at the door even now. Only later can she break free of the memory entombed here—and she washes the coffee cup.

> **WORK POINT:** look around your own room: what does it say about you—good or bad? Imagine that you have died, and that someone else is keeping this room as a shrine to your memory: which items would you want preserved? Which would you not?

Stock characters: libraries, labyrinths, bookshops

Treat buildings with respect, and they become characters in your fiction. To know and respect your building, it helps to have a clear notion of the geography of your story, at least in your head. Orhan Pamuk gives us a street map for finding *The Museum of Innocence* in Istanbul. Umberto Eco provides a plan of the abbey in *The Name of The Rose*, and the layout is important to the mystery, which culminates in a library in which the heroes are lost, and which is burning.

They are lost because the library is a labyrinth. Just as certain landscapes (thesea, thedesert) readily take on symbolic force in fiction, so certain interiors do the same. Labyrinths, with their history stretching back to ancient Crete, often appear in novels concerned with the mind and its darker recesses; besides *The Name of The Rose*, there is Lawrence Durrell's Mediterranean story *The Dark Labyrinth* and Ruth Rendell's *The Minotaur* [55] (again, there is a library, and a terrible fire). A related tradition is the bookshop,

---

[55] Written under her pseudonym Barbara Vine.

found in many mystery and thriller novels: there is one in John le Carré's *The Spy That Came In From The Cold*, one in Raymond Chandler's *The Big Sleep*, and one in *Night Train To Lisbon*. In Carlos Ruiz Zafon's *The Shadow of The Wind*, there is a combination of the two in the backstreets of old Barcelona, a vast Cemetery of Lost Books where forgotten volumes are preserved.

Such locations have a distinct character. The literary bookshop is a place of quiet, thoughtful enquiry, where slightly shabby people come to seek something, and meet strangers. The acoustic is muffled, with only the tinkling of the doorbell. There is an odour of dust (you can smell the past) and a vast quantity of secrets between covers, waiting to be opened. Chandler's bookshop in *The Big Sleep* is ironic, however: it's a fraud, a front for a vice racket.

Take some other rooms: how about the attic? In David Almond's *Skellig*, an angel lives there. What about the cellar? That is usually more sinister: John Fowles (*The Collector*), Steig Larsson (*The Girl With The Dragon Tattoo*) and more recently Emma Donoghue (*Room*)[56] have women imprisoned in cellars. Kitchens are where people congregate at parties, and are an excellent venue for murder and for sex, full of dangerous implements, stark theatrical lighting, and surfaces that are excitingly hard and cold.

Consider the normal expectations of any room, and play with these by undermining them: this will unsettle the reader, making them wonder what is going on, and introducing an undercurrent of tension or comedy. A bathroom should be clean: what if it is disgustingly dirty? What is behind us in the mirror that is not there when we turn? A bedroom should be warm and relaxing, but it may be comfortless: in *Mansfield Park*, the family at the big house treat Fanny badly; her kindly uncle Sir Thomas realises this because in the depths of winter there is no fire in her room. This tiny episode[57] is carefully placed, coming immediately before Sir Thomas

---

[56] Based on the grim true-life experiences of Natascha Kampusch and Elizabeth Fritzl.
[57] It occurs in Chapter XXXII.

is displeased with Fanny for refusing what seems a good offer of marriage. We shall see (Chapter Eleven) how people may be built up just before a crisis; Sir Thomas's kindness is reinforced moments before he criticizes Fanny, so we know that he is good-hearted really.

> **WORK POINT:** write a description of a perfectly charming basement, a sweet little garage or an oddly pretty utility room. What might it tell us about the people who inhabit that home? How might it contribute to their story?

Descriptions of settings should not be dumped into a novel like so much hardcore, but used dynamically—and if they are not working for your story, they shouldn't be there.

Summary points

- Don't describe interiors in isolation; link them to their human resonance.
- Evoke the effects (good and bad) that buildings have on their occupants. Is this a product of the building, or of the character's state of mind?
- The contents of a room may have both narrative and symbolic significance.
- Your description should include a wide range of sensory information: sounds, smells, textures …
- Buildings have a history. Things have happened here in the past: how do they affect the present?
- Play on the normal expectations of rooms, and subvert them.

11   People portrayed

In Chapter Five, we considered the conflicts that people face, conflicts that give rise to stories. But how does one go about portraying characters, making them vivid in the reader's imagination? If you fail to do that, then no amount of cunning plot devices will get your readers' sympathy. Readers engage with characters first, plots second.

The first question is: do *you* know the cast of your story?

How well do you know your characters?

It is sometimes recommended that when writing fiction you should know your main characters as thoroughly as someone you share a house with. Deborah Moggach has described how, before embarking on a new novel, she liked to "take each character out for a walk", placing them in different contexts to see how they would behave.[58] She added, however, that a person taken from a world close to one's own, perhaps someone similar to oneself, can be difficult to write about convincingly because—like an object held too close to the eye—they will not be in focus. They need to be held back a little. I experienced this when writing my novel *Poor Mercy*, concerning aid workers in Sudan—a job that I had done myself. The African characters, mostly invented from scratch, came easily. The people I had trouble with were the European aid workers, people like me.

In the mid-20th century, it was fashionable to debate whether one can even consider the lives of characters outside of the books or drama in which they appear: in the phrase of the French theorist Jacques Derrida, "There is nothing

---

[58] At the Arvon Foundation course we tutored together, at Moniack Mhor, Inverness-shire, in 2005.

outside the text". The Shakespearean critic L.C. Knights mocked the idea of characters living off the page (or stage) with an influential essay entitled, "*How many children had Lady Macbeth?*"

The question for fiction writers is a little different: does it actually help you, as the writer, to imagine the whole of your character's life? Some writers find that it does: Raymond Chandler claimed to know every detail of Philip Marlowe's life, wardrobe and apartment. But do not confuse these two things: what you, as the author, need to know about your character, and what your readers need to know. What readers look for is not psychoanalysis, but a story.

Some writers compile a check-list of personal attributes for each character. The list might include their private history, their school and employment career, their politics, their taste in music, the books they have on their bedside table (if any), their choice of mobile phone ringtone, their detailed physical description, their hobbies and pets … and so on. An inventory like this may help you to keep an image of your character clear in your mind. It may also help if you face the difficulty of characters who are too like yourself; it can assist the process of setting them apart. And if you are writing any sort of serial—whether in prose fiction or for television or radio—then it can be important to have a reference set of attributes for characters. This is the case in long-running soap operas, written by many different hands, where there will be something called "the bible", used to check the colour of Eddie Grundy's hair, and where he was born.

For the novelist, however, what is important is not whether you know your protagonist's ring-tone and date of birth, but how well you know their behaviour and motives. A neat instance is Henry James's novel *The Awkward Age*, which concerns a young girl's awakening to the devious emotional world of adults. But what exactly *is* "the awkward age", and just how old *is* the girl, Nanda? The other characters are not sure:

> 'She's only seventeen, or eighteen, I suppose …'
> 'Isn't she eighteen?'
> 'I have to think. Wouldn't it be nearer twenty?'

That is all that is ever said. What matters about Nanda's age is: it's awkward.

At this point, you may like to glance ahead to the discussion of short stories, and all the information you do *not* need in a narrative (p. 201). The springs of a story are tension, desire, conflict, want *versus* need. Never mind hair colour: you should be able to challenge yourself—at any point in your book—with the question: *What does my character want, at this moment?* What is it makes them want this? Is it just their present circumstances (the advancing crocodiles, the glint of gold), or is it the dreams from their past that haunt them? That is what you must be able to answer, and that is what constitutes "knowing your character".

> **WORK POINT:** take any novel or drama and consider the same characters with radically different attributes: make the young heroine a seventy-year-old—why not? Does it make a real, or only a superficial difference? What if you change all the personal details? Could the story still work?

What do you give your readers?

How much use is an "inventory" of character attributes to readers? How far will it bring a character alive?

In certain genre fiction—crime and thrillers, for instance—a crudely drawn personality may be sufficient. You may get away with creating characters by slipping in part of your check list: age, appearance (healthy or otherwise), occupation, dress, a few personal tastes and political leanings, a particular car, a couple of foibles … *Voil*á! You have a character, of a sort. In most fiction, however, this will be too crude for anything other than minor figures.

Remember the intricate relation of character and conflict, of motivation and story, and make sure that the image that you give your readers of your main characters is a *dynamic* aspect of your writing. It must work for you.

Let's look at some ways in which this may be done.

A matter of appearances—men

In the early 20th century, novelists such as Arnold Bennett wrote fiction which was resolutely realist. It described appearances and reality. It looked outward rather than inward. Virginia Woolf objected to this; she protested against the notion of creating character through externals, through endless description: "'Describe cancer. Describe calico. Describe …'—but I cried, 'Stop! Stop!'"[59]

But can personality never be revealed by appearances? What if characters are themselves bothered by self-image, as so many people are? How about this, from our new novel *On The Shore*:

> Right: time to prepare for confronting Gibson at the bank. I shall wear my River Island black suit with the Nehru collar, which has a look of (dare I say) almost mystical clarity of purpose. I shall wear a cool blue shirt, and the fawn Bally shoes with their whiplash laces and their lightweight leather—for today I am light on my feet. I shall have a handkerchief in my breast pocket, dark blue, and the charcoal socks with sharks on them. I am trim, I am agile. Today I shall be making a killing.

What impression is our hero wanting to give? Does it strike you as faintly menacing—or does the self-consciousness undermine that menace?

It is interesting to see how much, or how little, different authors describe the physical appearance of characters. This may be something as simple as making the villain of *The Da Vinci Code* an albino monk; he is immediately marked out as strange; the visual image can be instantly accessed by the reader.[60]

---

[59] In a talk given in Cambridge in 1924.

[60] Be careful, however, to avoid chauvinistic stereotyping. In the best selling novel about the Afghan Taliban, *The Kite Runner*, the villain is an Afghan but with a German mother, so that he can be given blue eyes and fair hair, marking him as a quasi-Nazi.

I sometimes ask students to close their eyes and take a snap image, unedited by second thoughts, of a character that I am about to name: Lady Macbeth. It is remarkable how consistent the images turn out to be: she is usually a slim woman with straight, dark hair, soberly dressed … It is a stereotype, clearly, derived from any number of theatre productions and perhaps *One Hundred & One Dalmatians.* Shakespeare's text gives us nothing to go on, and we could imagine Lady Macbeth as we please. But we stay true to type.

You may protest: fiction is different! But in even the most nuanced of literary fiction, character description often matches our expectations. Here, from the beginning of *The Master of Petersburg*, is J.M. Coetzee's description of Dostoevsky getting out of a horse-drawn cab:

> The passenger steps out. He is a man in late middle age, bearded and stooped, with a high forehead and heavy eyebrows that lend him an air of sober self-absorption. He wears a dark suit of somewhat démodé cut.

This is not so far from a description of Coetzee himself. Dostoevsky is not actually named in the novel, and this man could have been described in any way. But Coetzee does not disappoint our expectations of what a somewhat ascetic, rather troubled Russian intellectual ought to look like. We need no more, and he keeps it short.

This most sophisticated novelist is content to use simple external features to place his character before us. Authors may have in their heads a clear image of their subjects—as did Enid Blyton, who once described[61] how she would sit with her typewriter on her knees, shut her eyes and find her characters standing there perfectly clear in her mind's eye, right down to every detail of their appearance and their names (although only the forename; she claimed to get the surnames out of the phone book later). But if you look in the Famous Five books for descriptions of the children, you'll find very little except for George, the girl who wants to be a boy, and who wears her hair short.

---

[61] In a letter to Professor Peter McKellar, February 1953.

It is where characters confound expectations that description becomes most interesting and engaging. Here is our first sight of a very un-stereotypic pirate captain, from Richard Hughes' *A High Wind In Jamaica*:

> [Captain Jonsen] was a clumsy great fellow, with a sad silly face. He was bulky, yet so ill-proportioned one got no impression of power. He was modestly dressed in a drab shore-going suit; he was newly shaven, and his sparse hair was pomaded so that it lay in a few dark ribbons across his baldish top. But all this shore-decency of appearance only accentuated his big splodgy brown hands, stained and scarred and corned with his calling. Moreover, instead of boots he wore a pair of gigantic heelless slippers in the Moorish manner, which he must have sliced with a knife out of some dead sea-boots. Even his great spreading feet could hardly keep them on, so that he was obliged to walk at the slowest of shuffles, flop-flop along the deck. He stooped, as if always afraid of banging his head on something, and carried the backs of his hands forward, like an orang-utan …
>
> When he spoke at last, it was with a soft German accent:
>
> "Excuse me," he began, "but would you have the goodness to lend me a few stores?" … (Meanwhile his men had the hatches off and were preparing to help themselves to everything in the ship.)

Beautiful women

So much for men. Now let's consider some beautiful women:

> Emma Woodhouse, handsome, clever and rich, with a comfortable home and a happy disposition, seemed to unite some of the best blessings of existence, and had lived nearly twenty-one years in the world with very little to vex her.

"Handsome": that is all the description Jane Austen ever gives us of Emma. It will do; we can fill in the rest. Wouldn't you agree, though, that someone described in such satisfactory terms is heading for trouble? She going to be vexed, surely—so this description is indeed dynamic.

An effective description contains within it features that will play a role in the narrative. Here is Tolstoy's first description of Anna Karenina getting off a train in Moscow, as seen by her future lover Count Vronsky:

> The trained insight of a Society man enabled Vronsky with a single glance to decide that she belonged to the best Society. He apologised for being in her way and was about to enter the carriage, but he felt compelled to have another look at her, not because she was very beautiful nor because of the elegance and modest grace of her whole figure, but because he saw in her sweet face as she passed him something specially tender and kind. He looked round, and she too turned her head. Her bright grey eyes which seemed dark because of their black lashes rested for a moment on his face as if recognising him, and then turned to the passing crowd evidently in search of some one. In that short look Vronksy had time to notice the subdued animation that enlivened her face and seemed to flutter between her bright eyes and a scarcely perceptible smile which curved her rosy lips. It was as if an excess of vitality so filled her whole being that it betrayed itself against her will, now in her smile, now in the light of her eyes. She deliberately tried to extinguish that light in her eyes, but it shone in spite of her in her faint smile.

Tolstoy says, quite specifically, that it is not Anna's beauty that catches Vronsky's eye; rather, it is the qualities that shine out of her. It is also, however, the constraints. Here we have set up the conflict between a young, vivacious spirit and a sense of repression, and of propriety only just in control. It is that visible "excess of vitality" that will drive Anna's tragedy, not the colour of her dress. The conflict is clearly visible to Vronsky, even in the "bright grey eyes which seemed dark". Remember that this is Anna as seen by the man who will—against all polite codes—become her lover. We are learning about Vronsky too, and about the relationship that is coming.

This is dynamic description.

Public image, of course, may be as important to women as to our snappily dressed man heading off to meet Gibson at the bank. *The Leopard* is Giuseppe di Lampedusa's novel of old Sicily.[62] The Leopard himself is the Prince of Salina, the epitome of ancient lineage and exquisite manners. He holds a dinner at his palace to which he invites the local mayor. In the eyes of the Prince's family, the mayor is a vulgar jumped-up peasant, new money, small and coarse and comical and very badly dressed for dinner. His tail coat is a disaster of inept tailoring, and he is wearing (oh, horror!) buttoned boots. The Prince's family smother their laughs and their embarrassment.

But in behind the mayor comes his daughter Angelica. The palace nobility are speechless. She is stunning. She is tall and blonde, with faintly cruel green eyes, a creamy skin and a strawberry mouth. She moves in such a way that her gorgeous white dress swings slowly about her. She seems utterly confident of her own loveliness … Later, they discover that poor Angelica was about to pass out with fear.

Here, the detail of appearance has work to do: it depicts the social gulf between the mayor and the Prince, a driving force of much of what follows; it emphasises the impact of Angelica (another mainspring of the story); and it sets up the paradox of her nervousness—that is, her humanity.

Again: dynamic description.

---

[62] *Il Gattopardo* (The Leopard) was published in 1961, shortly after Lampedusa's death, and was an international best-seller. The author came from the Sicilian nobility himself. The novel became in 1963 a celebrated film by Luchino Visconti, starring Burt Lancaster as the Prince and Claudia Cardinale as Angelica.

Appearance may also be ironic. Early in *Madame Bovary*, Emma is described through the eyes of her foolish husband Charles and her would-be lover Léon. Charles is delighted with her sweet virtue, her obedience, her neat housework. Léon is smitten with how pale, thin and saintly she appears, with her silence, her remoteness. The village gossips admire her thrift, and even the pharmacist remarks, "She's got class!" What none of them realise is that Emma is being torn apart by sexual lust for Léon and for a craving for money that she struggles to suppress. They are completely fooled by appearances.

A rather different example: this is from the first description of Lisbeth Salander, the heroine of Steig Larsson's violent thriller *The Girl With The Dragon Tattoo*. She is employed at a firm called Milton Security:

> Milton's image was one of conservative stability. Salander fitted into this picture about as well as a buffalo at a boat show … a pale, anorexic young woman who had hair as short as a fuse, and a pierced nose and eyebrows. She had a wasp tattoo about two centimetres long on her neck … [and] dragon tattoo on her left shoulder blade. She was a natural redhead, but she dyed her hair raven black. She looked as though she had just emerged from a week-long orgy with a gang of hard-rockers … She had a wide mouth, a small nose, and high cheek-bones that gave her an almost Asian look. Her movements were quick and spidery … Sometimes she wore black lipstick, and in spite of the tattoos and the pierced nose and eyebrows she was … well … attractive. It was inexplicable.

Everything reinforces the idea of Lisbeth as an outsider, a walking paradox, filled with a disdain for Swedish social norms but also with a relentless energy for justice. Notice the vocabulary: *wasp, raven, fuse, dragon, blade, spidery, orgy, gang, hard, red, black, pierced* …. This fits with the drive of the story, which concerns the tensions within that society, the gross abuse and murder of women, and Lisbeth's single-minded pursuit of abusers. The story will make full use of what has been prepared in this description.

Finally, beauty may be a set-up for something very different. William Styron's *Sophie's Choice* concerns a Polish survivor of Auschwitz, now in Brooklyn. She is young, she is very beautiful—although her precise beauty is conventional. But at one startling moment, quite early in the book, her admirer Stingo catches her unawares in front of a mirror. Her lovely face seems to have collapsed ... for she is not wearing the false teeth that, as a severely malnourished camp victim, she now needs. She looks like a death mask; in this moment, her tragic story is prefigured.

You will see that, in most of these descriptions, there is a conflict between appearance and reality, or between what appearance says about a character, and what that character really wants. The hero of *On The Shore* is dressing with a bravado he does not entirely feel. Anna Karenina betrays a vivacity at odds with social constraints. Emma Bovary looks like "class" but is consumed by lust. Lisbeth Salander looks like "a buffalo at a boat show"—and so on. Each author has used description to make vivid a tension within the character, and that is what makes them crackle with life.

Where—or when—to describe a character?

Pretty much as soon as they are introduced, no? That is what we had with Emma, Anna, Angelica and Lisbeth, not to mention Dostoevsky. Remember the very first time we see Rick Blaine in *Casablanca*: we see only his hands on the table; we note that he wears gold cufflinks; that he holds a cigarette; that he is playing chess against himself; that there is a glass of brandy by the chessboard; that he is given a cheque to countersign. In this snapshot we learn immediately about his intelligence, his style, his edgy solitariness even among good company, and his power—all before we even see his face.

So: description on first meeting? Not necessarily. You may find it positioned elsewhere.

Pascal Mercier, the Swiss author of *Night Train To Lisbon*, gives very few descriptions of his protagonist, a distinguished teacher of languages and philology in Bern. Only when Gregorius takes that night train and actually reaches Lisbon is he portrayed. There, he suddenly feels entirely out of place—and looks it:

> The bar was full of well-dressed men from an office building next door. Gregorius looked at his new face in the mirror, then the whole figure … The baggy corduroy trousers, the rough turtleneck and the old anorak contrasted with the many tailored jackets, the matching shirts and ties around him. Nor did they suit the new glasses, not at all …

In this novel, a physical description has suddenly become useful, well into the story. Previously, it had little relevance.

In *Troilus & Criseyde*, Geoffrey Chaucer tells the story of the Trojan lovers that Shakespeare was to rework in his *Troilus & Cressida*. Unlike Shakespeare's cynical tale, Chaucer's version is, as usual, warm and humane. Divided into five books, it goes as follows:

WORK POINT: reading this summary, consider where you would position a glowing description of Criseyde.

Book one

Criseyde is a young Trojan noblewoman who is terrified of the Greeks besieging her city, and who has no one to protect her. Prince Troilus sees her and falls madly in love. He begs Criseyde's uncle Pandare[63] for help.

Book two

Pandare gets to work, suggesting to Criseyde that Troilus is just the man to look after her. She falls in love too.

---

[63] "Pandarus" in Shakespeare—the origin of the verb *to pander* to someone else's desires.

Book three

Pandare has Troilus pretend to be dying of a broken heart. Although fearful for her good name, Criseyde agrees to visit—and they end up in bed, enraptured.

Book four

Catastrophe! There's a prisoner exchange, and Criseyde must go to the Greeks. She and Troilus swear to be true, and swap rings and handkerchiefs. But, in the Greek camp, Criseyde's terror returns.

Book five

Criseyde cannot help it: desperate for a new protector, she gives herself to the Greek, Diomed. Distraught, Troilus is finally slain in battle.

So: where in this story would a close physical description of the lovely Criseyde be of most use? In Book One, where Troilus sees her in the temple and falls head over heels? In Book Two, where they become more and more infatuated? Or in Book Three, at the climax of the romance, where they lie naked in each other's arms gazing in ecstasy? Perhaps in Book Four, with Troilus looking at the lovely woman that he is about to lose?

No: it comes towards the end, well into Book Five,[64] immediately before Criseyde betrays Troilus in that despicable, craven way. Why?

The Book Five description is detailed and penetrating. To begin with, Criseyde is portrayed physically: she is slim and lightly built, with a charming way of letting her hair fall down her back with a gold thread tied through it; her eyes are particularly lovely, although there is a curious joining of her eyebrows. Then her character is dwelt on: sober and wise, unpretentious, well-spoken, kindly and generous, free-spirited and sympathetic … but "slydynge of corage". There, in that last wonderful phrase, is the crunch: neither her beauty nor her virtues can protect Criseyde from her own fearfulness.

---

[64] *Troilus & Criseyde*, Book Five, ll. 806–826.

And we are told all this just before the final betrayal. Chaucer—with his usual compassion, and also his unerring dramatic sense—makes Criseyde as warm and appealing as possible just before her crime. By doing so, he makes subsequent events far more affecting and human. Because we have every possible feeling for Criseyde, we care what happens.

You will find this technique, of reinforcing a character just before a crisis, used again and again. At the end of *Madame Bovary*, Emma—whose self-indulgence, snobbery and romanticism has caused such chaos—finally chooses suicide and goes to the pharmacy to obtain arsenic. Just as she decides on this, Flaubert describes her in generous terms that he has never used before, speaking of her 'heroic resolve', while the pharmacist's assistant is startled by her physical appearance:

> He gazed at her, astonished by her face pale against the black night. To him she seemed wonderfully beautiful, as majestic as an apparition from some other world. He had no idea what she wanted, but he was filled with a terrible foreboding.

Acts of kindness

There are other ways to build up a character before a crisis. Look again at the outline of *Casablanca* (p.78). In Sequence Six, Rick comes up against the crunch decision: will he do the decent thing and help Victor Laszlo? Or will he remain embittered and selfish? Things look bad; he refuses to help. At this point, however, he does two very honourable things which lift him high in our estimation: he helps a desperate couple of young Bulgarian refugees by contriving to have them win a large sum of money at the roulette table; and dangerously he permits Laszlo to counter the Nazis' military songs by leading the band and all the customers in the *Marseillaise*. In these two moments of decency, we know the real Rick Blaine—and we feel confident of how he will decide.

In William Styron's *Sophie's Choice*, the visual image of Sophie is clear from early on; she's gorgeous. However, there is a similar device near the end. Sophie has been portrayed through the eyes of Stingo, who is obsessed with her, lusting for her delectable body. But Stingo is in fact a virgin and sexually inept. Before she finally departs from him, Sophie relieves him of that torturing virginity. It is a scene of frantic eroticism, but is also a parting act of compassion. We—Stingo and readers—experience Sophie at her loveliest, just before her final disaster.

People and their little ways—using tags and motifs

Such subtle, powerful descriptions are usually kept for principle characters. For secondary persons it is often enough to have them summed up in a pithy phrase. In *The Reef*, Edith Wharton—an American but, like Henry James, besotted with pre-WW1 Europe—has a character of occasional narrative importance, a bossy, rather loud and stupid woman, who is summed up as having "a mind entirely devoid of echoes, notwithstanding its vacuity". That is the sort of put-down one doesn't forget in a hurry, something one remembers whenever she re-occurs.

Sometimes a secondary character will be given a tag that enables them to be identified whenever they pop up to do their bit: this might be something physical—an item of clothing, a mannerism, an irritating tendency to click ballpoint pens—or it could be a catchphrase. You will notice these often in film: in *Some Like It Hot*, one of the mobsters is always chewing a toothpick, while in *Butch Cassidy And The Sundance Kid*, the lawman pursuing Butch and Sundance can always be identified from a distance by his white hat. In fiction—without the instant availability of something visible on screen—a single mannerism may be more useful: a turn of phrase, an irritating habit, a physical trait. Rather than load all your cast with detailed characterisation, try such identifying tags.

Principals may also be given a marker of this sort, just as Wagner introduced the idea of a musical *Leitmotif* to identify each of the main figures in his operas. Many fictional characters can be epitomised in very few attributes: Inspector Morse, for instance, with his endless Wagner recordings and his meanness about buying drinks. Or the would-be novelist X. Trapnel in Anthony Powell's *Books Do Furnish A Room*, an author with no money who insists on going everywhere about London by taxi (in a daydream about his coming fame and grandeur). In my own *Poor Mercy*, set among aid workers in Sudan, the team leader Xavier is given a list of attributes which somehow *don't quite* sum him up. In his own eyes, he is characterised by one particular fear: thirst:

> Here lay Xavier Hopkins, Field Director, charged with devising systems for forecasting and preventing ghastly famine in Darfur Province: thirty-eight years old, six-foot-two, pale skin and thin hair, fastidious, slightly Catholic, well-experienced in the realms of Aid, an MA in African history and terrified of going into the desert with insufficient drinking water. A poor linguist but a sharp mind, so it said in his employer's files. A gentle chap, people agreed. Out of his depth, he himself suspected.

> Xavier's fear of dehydration recurs throughout the novel.

Giveaway moments

The most over-used phrase in writing workshops is: "Show, don't tell." A good novelist seeks out a balance between showing and telling. In film, it is far better to reveal a personality by something that they do than by hearing them talk, but in this respect, fiction and drama are very different: the novelist must be prepared to get inside the head and to examine a character's thinking.

This does not mean, however, that we should separate thinking from actions. One of the simplest ways to bring a character to life is to have them observe an event (however trivial), and to react and think about it.

Emma Bovary is a would-be social climber who longs to mix with the best society. Flaubert sends her to a ball at a château, the home of a noble family with intoxicating names like Jean-Antoine-Henry-Guy d'Andervilliers de la Vaubyessard. Emma is thrilled; she takes infinite care with her dress, she is mortified by her oafish husband's lack of refinement. But she is also perplexed by a tiny moment at dinner:

> Madame Bovary was surprised to see that a number of the ladies had not tucked their gloves into their wine glasses.

Emma knows that a polite lady does not drink wine, and that putting her glove in her glass will stop the butler pouring for her. What Emma doesn't understand is that really classy ladies have the self-confidence that allows them to drink what they like. The gulf between her pretensions and the behaviour of those born to class is made clear in one giveaway moment.

So: we are told about Emma by her reaction to one little incident. Raymond Chandler takes his detective Philip Marlowe to the Los Angeles house of a newly wealthy young man; the house is luxurious. In a moment of nervous irritation, the young man spits onto his own deep-pile carpet. Marlowe observes—and knows everything he needs to know about this character.

Language and register

Characters reveal themselves the moment they open their mouths. No amount of pretentious behaviour can cover up "common" speech or an accent. John le Carré's *The Tailor of Panama* concerns a man who has concocted a fake personality for himself as a Savile Row bespoke outfitter of the highest class. Mr Pendel is actually nothing of the sort: he is a former convict who learned his tailoring not on Savile Row but in prison. The giveaway is his accent. He is, we are told, "branded on the tongue."

Internal speech matters too: the thought-language of our languidly superior art dealer in *On The Shore* will differ from that of the working class painter-genius visiting the gallery, and they will use a different "register"—levels of diction, or degrees of formality—to assert their status or perhaps their contempt for status:

> De Vere surveyed Gibson's stubbly pate, the appalling synthetic smock besmirched with yestereen's bolognese, the disagreeable odour of turpentine melded with a veritable miasma from the nether-oxter.
>
> 'Oh, mercy,' winced De Vere.
>
> Gibson saw the wince, and thought, 'What a total plonker.'

Keep the vocabulary appropriate to the character. If you have a seven year-old girl wondering how to escape from a locked bedroom without being heard, *don't* have her say to herself: "The prime consideration would be to minimise the cacophony from the shattered glazing." This is inappropriate not only as the language of her thoughts: it should not be the language in which you discuss her situation either, even as a detached Third Person narrator.

A character will be coloured not just by description, actions, thoughts and speech, but even by the prose style that you use in their vicinity. Here is the opening sentence of Henry James's *The Wings of The Dove*. For preference, read this aloud, slowly:

> She waited, Kate Croy, for her father to come in, but he kept her unconscionably, and there were moments at which she showed herself, in the glass over the mirror, a face positively pale with the irritation that had brought her to the point of going away without sight of him.

The prose rhythm itself reflects the tension in Kate: notice the awkward positioning of her name, and then the long unravelling of the last clause, spooling out of her like her irritation. Contrast it with the opening words from William Rivière's novel *Kate Caterina*:

She had harvest coloured hair, and brown eyes, and her name was Kate Fenn …

We are only fourteen words in, but already everything about this woman is different. The name is suggestive of an East Anglian landscape (which is indeed where she comes from) compared to Kate Croy, a name with a quite different feel. The colours imply a mellow warmth. The sentence sways in a gentle, watery way, unlike the nervous energy Henry James associates with Kate Croy.

In *Poor Mercy* I attempted an effect not unlike James, using broken phrasing and awkward punctuation to convey hesitation. Here, a Sudanese woman is anxiously informing her husband of an invitation that she fears he won't like it. Again, try reading it aloud, noting the punctuation:

> 'Beloved? I'd like to invite some friends,' his mother said, one day, at dinner, 'to our home'.

Sure enough, he hates it. All these things—physical appearance, tiny moments of behaviour, little reactions, speech patterns, names, even punctuation—are part of your armoury for bringing a character alive.

A last thought on character

In the early 19th century, Samuel Taylor Coleridge wrote profoundly of the creative process, distinguishing between what he called "fancy" and "imagination". Fancy was the assembling of parts, sticking bits together in an amusing concoction. Imagination was something far more special, something charged with an inner life and spirit of its own.[65]

For novelists, this distinction is important. While the "inventory" approach is easy, it will never be more than limited in its results. It places emphasis on aspects of the character that are "non-dynamic" in terms of storytelling.

---

[65] In his *Biographia Literaria* (1817), a personal history of his literary thinking.

It forgets that fiction concerns players in a drama, in whom no attribute is truly relevant if it is not linked to motivation, or does not drive the story, or does not reinforce the theme. If you try to construct a figure by using a check list, you run the risk that you will create something dead, a fiction-robot, a creation that can be plugged into any circumstance and turned on.

I repeatedly emphasise in this book the notion that every aspect of fiction should be seen as *dynamic*—working for the story.

Summary points

- In general, it is far more important to know how your characters think than how they look.
- The details that matter are those that reveal dynamic aspects of character—aspects that are going to play a part in the story.
- Incongruous and surprising features are much more interesting and useful than the conventional, and more worth bothering with.
- How much does physical appearance matter to your characters themselves?
- Position your description where it is of most use. This is not necessarily at first meeting.
- Use identifying tags and typifying behaviour for secondary characters.
- Characterise through speech—but also through any language associated with the character, even in a Third Person narration.
- An inventory of attributes is a short-cut to a dead character. Personality must take life from within.

12 **Fertile plots**

If you search the internet, you will find people who will sell you (or even give you) a story plot. This is not new: before World War One there were agencies advertising such a service: two shillings for a simple outline, three shillings for a better one. But if you want to tell your own story rather than someone else's, you'll need to consider plotting carefully.

We've looked at narrative structure in Chapter Seven. Plot is another aspect of the matter, and concerns the questions, the mysteries and all the other ways in which you maintain interest in a story.

Mysteries and questions

It is traditional at this point to quote E.M. Forster,[66] so for a change let's paraphrase him. What is the difference between the following?

- A woman leaves her home, and then a neighbour leaves home.
- A woman leaves her home, and her neighbour goes after her.
- A woman disappears, then a neighbour disappears also, and no one knows why until they learn that the neighbour was in love with the woman.

The first of these is merely a set of events. The second establishes a causal link that turns the events into a story. The third version is (in Forster's terms) a plot capable of "high development" because it contains a mystery. Our version is a slight improvement on Forster's, which involves

---

[66] In particular, his lectures given at Cambridge University and published (in 1927) as *Aspects of the Novel: Lecture 5—The Plot*. Forster's remarks are quoted in many books on creative writing.

a king dying and his queen then dying of grief, and which does rather close down the story. In ours, there is plenty of story still to come. The plotting questions are: *how* was the truth discovered? And *what* will happen next?

If you look again at three-act structure (Chapter Seven) you'll see that, with each sequence or part of the story, a series of questions arises. These questions may be to do with discovering the truth about the past, or with how to cope with a present difficulty or a danger that faces us in the future. Each question will set us on a new line of enquiry, at the end of which we will have some sort of answer. But we will also now have a *new* question which will send us off again, and in a different direction.

It may be that the later answers we find undermine the earlier answers: that's to say, we may *think* that in the first enquiry we've solved the problem, until facts emerge in the next sequence which demonstrate that we were wrong, and must think again.

The key here is: "facts emerge": Plotting is largely a matter of how we discover information, when we discover it, and the consequences of discovery. The essential thing is to be clear: *What is the question?*

So: what *is* the question?

This may seem obvious, but writers often get it wrong when sorting out plots, and the question may not be the obvious one. In the Van der Valk novels of Nicolas Freeling, set in 1960s Holland, we have a series of crime mysteries, sometimes (not always) involving a murder. But these are not "whodunits"; there is usually little mystery as to the criminal's identity. In *Gun Before Butter*, a wealthy man is found stabbed to death in an Amsterdam flat. Piet Van der Valk does not follow many clues to the murderer; he just thinks of someone he knows, and is right. Indeed, we know who the murderer is in advance, because we are introduced to her through a number of small incidents long before the crime occurs. Van der Valk gets to know and to like her; then comes the killing. So, the question is: *why* did Lucienne Engelbert stab

Meinard Stam? On the way, the sub-questions are: what was Stam's complicated business? Who was his *alter ego*? How did he and Lucienne meet, and what attracted them to each other? Why did she feel betrayed? It is a romantic mystery as much as anything else. In the process of answering all these questions, a complex portrait of both characters is built up as Van der Valk gathers information. What makes the plot is the obstacles that get in the way of gathering that information and revealing the truth.

And here is an important realisation: the degree of complexity of any plot is arbitrary—or at least, you can make it just as complex as you please, but you do not have to. You may decide that you have too much plot; it can leave no room for characters to develop, or for the reader to think. You *could* present most of the key information in a discovered diary, with no difficulty for anyone in working it out. So, hesitate before you pile complications into your story. In *Gun Before Butter*, Van der Valk discovers many aspects of the tale with relative ease. Freeling *could* have made it far more difficult; he *could* have set up many more obstacles, just as many as he liked. He *could* have spun the plot out as long as he wanted, into a very long novel. But Freeling was interested in other questions: character and motivation, European cultural complexities, and love.

This will apply to literary novels also. The essential plot of Henry James's *The Wings of The Dove* is, as we have seen, that two young people contrive to get a rich dying woman to leave them all her money by suggesting that there is deep love between the sick woman and the young man. But by the end, the question is not "Will Kate and Densher get Milly's money?" but "What will they do to Milly and themselves in the process?" Therefore, what the plot must deliver is information about character change, not about trickery.

Orhan Pamuk's complex *My Name Is Red* begins with that corpse in a well speculating as to how he came to be there, and warning the reader that there has been a conspiracy. But what obsesses the dead man's ghost is "an appalling conspiracy against our religion, our traditions and the way we see the world." It is to do with art and high culture, and the battle between eastern and western values. Only when he has unravelled these knotty problems will the victim understand *why* he has been killed, and thus by whom. Understand the question, and you will understand what needs to be revealed by the plot.

Gabriel Garcia Marquez's novel *Chronicle of A Death Foretold* begins with a clear statement of what will happen at the end:

> The day on which they were going to kill him, Santiago Nasar rose at 5.30 in the morning …

The conclusion of the story is not in doubt: Santiago ends up dead. We know that from the outset. The question is: *why?* (He is being pursued for deflowering a girl—but did he do it?).

Only when you are sure of your question can you decide what information and pointers need to be provided.

> **WORK POINT:** try writing the back-cover "blurb" of a few novels that you know. You have a maximum of seventy words. So: what is the nub of the story? What is the question that drives it?

Pacing the information

What is the style and the pace of your novel, and how fast will information be revealed? You have to be sure of what you are trying to achieve: a speedy thriller, or a meditation upon a theme? Pamuk's *My Name Is Red* will disappoint anyone looking for a thriller, because much of it is taken up with long meditations on the nature of Ottoman art.

Do not confuse pace of plot with pace of action. We have all seen films in which there is a great deal of fighting or chasing or sex, but not a lot of story (and they are dull as a result). The same goes for novels. Pacing the *plot* is a matter of how fast you reveal information. You can see that, in three-act structure, the process of learning is spread out through the sequences, especially through Act Two. At the end of Act

One, the main question has been established: in Act Two, we are looking for answers and gathering information. In Act Three, little new information is collected: it's now a matter of how things work out. Glance again at the outline of *Casablanca* (p. 78) and note how key items of information are steadily revealed throughout the narrative.

If you want a faster-paced story, do you wish this to be uniformly hectic or something more carefully varied? Again, consider three-act structure: even literary fiction may start with fast moving events in Act One; the catalyst in Gordimer's *The Pickup* occurs in the first sentence. Then things may ease off a little, as we get to know the characters better. As Act Two progresses, the pace picks up. At each turning point, the stakes are raised. In mystery stories (including *My Name Is Red*), towards the climax another body is discovered—indicating that the killer is on the loose and prepared to kill again. The pressure is on; information will now be coming thick and fast.

Cruder writing will dispense with any gradation, starting with events, proceeding with more events and continuing with an unvarying succession of events—and this is tedious. Stories, whether in novels or in film, need variation in pacing, or the audience will just feel battered and, fairly soon, bored. Readers want to be able to think as they read. So, build the pace towards an overall climax, but provide variation and build at other points also.

Beware of a pitfall: writers are sometimes advised that not only the overall structure of the story should build towards a climax, but that each scene or sequence of scenes should also have, on a smaller scale, a rising action. There is a danger here: a succession of scenes each of which builds to a climax and then slows, builds up again and slows, builds again … this can produce its own mechanical monotony, without organic flow. Here is one of the important differences between novels and drama: in fiction, there is room for nothing happening at all, except reflection.

Take care to distribute the gathering of information in a way that maintains interest, and give readers an opportunity to consider what is happening; have the characters ponder sometimes; have them restate the main question or new questions that have arisen, and have them contemplate the new obstacles. This way, you not only achieve a more satisfactory variety of pace, but you allow the reader to empathise with each character's dilemmas, and to see the full implications of the choices they must make.

One of the crucial decisions affecting the distribution of information is your choice of time frame.

Time frames

Georg Simmel, in his essay on *The Adventure*,[67] suggested that adventures have certain defining characteristics, one of which is a definite time-span—a clear beginning and end. Many stories reflect this when they commence with a statement on the lines of: "I didn't know where to start this story, until friends told me to start at the beginning."[68] It is essential to have a clear notion of the time span of your story, and the organisation of time within it.

If you look back at our "disappearing woman" paraphrase of Forster, you will notice that we enter the story in the middle: the plot is precipitated by the disappearances, but the love will have pre-existed that. There are clearly future developments coming, and also further discoveries to be made about the past.

At what point do we enter your story? In conventional detective novels (never mind *Gun Before Butter*), we arrive well into the sequence of events, since there generally has been a crime already committed to give the detective something to investigate. This applies to many other narratives, for instance *Sophie's Choice* and *Wuthering Heights*. Emily Brontë begins *Wuthering Heights* near to the conclusion, with the buffoonish Mr Lockwood encountering both the ghost of Catherine Linton and a near-deranged Heathcliff.

---

[67] See Chapter Two.
[68] See, for instance, the opening of Stevenson's *Treasure Island*, quoted on p. 28 above.

Badly shaken, he starts to question Nelly Dean, the old housekeeper. Nelly sits down with her knitting, delighted to oblige. Well now:

> Before I came to live here, she commenced, waiting no further invitation to her story; I was almost always at Wuthering Heights …

And she takes us quickly back into the past. Eventually we return to the point where we entered, in time to see the final act played out with Heathcliff's ghastly death.

Other narratives start even later in the story. Thornton Wilder's *Bridge of San Luis Rey* begins in 1714 with a group of travellers in Peru killed by a collapsing Inca rope bridge; the story goes back further into the past to tell us what brought them there, returning at the end to the catastrophe and a church service for the victims.

In each case there is a reason for delving into the past: the detective needs to solve a case; Mr Lockwood needs his nightmare explained away. The collapse of the Inca bridge is witnessed by a monk, Brother Juniper, who tries to discover God's will behind the catastrophe, investigates the story in depth and writes a fat book on the subject (unwisely: at the end of the novel, both Brother Juniper and his book are burned for heresy).

Garcia Marquez's *One Hundred Years of Solitude* begins with a man facing a firing squad, thinking back to the day his father took him to see ice for the first time. In the course of the novel, we cover generations of a community's history before returning to the present moment. An extreme example comes in a famous short story, *An Occurrence At Owl Creek Bridge* by Ambrose Bierce. During the American Civil War, a man is led out onto a bridge to be hanged. At the last moment he dives into the water, swims for his life as the soldiers shoot, and after hair-raising adventures makes it to his home, only to die suddenly just as he reaches the door … and we realise that all this escape has gone through his mind in the split second between being pushed off the bridge and the rope tightening about his neck.

> **WORK POINT:** once again, take a few novels that you
> know. What is the time frame? When (in the story) do
> they begin? How do they explore the past, if at all?

Bookending

A particular form of time structure is known as "bookending".
In this, we start with an event in the present day—perhaps
quite trivial—which provokes someone to recall the past.
At the end of the novel we return to the present, thinking
about what we have learned: the two short present-day
sections act as "bookends" supporting the tale from the past.
The initiating event might be a funeral at which you meet
a stranger who says: let me tell you the truth about your
father's life. Or anything else that prompts the protagonist to
think about the past or to learn about it.

Michael Frayn's novel *Spies* begins with a middle-aged
man walking down a street in which he smells privet hedges;
the scent provokes sad memories, as a result of which we
learn a sorry history—and finally return to the present to
think about it. Bookending can be a simple way of starting a
story: the discovery of a cache of letters reveals a mystery, for
instance. But it can also have particular effects on the tone;
it announces: "This is a learning experience. You thought
you understood the past? You were wrong. Now you shall
be told." At the end of the process, the narrator is older and
wiser, and so are we.

This is an effective means of heightening poignancy:
Spies is an example. We have a narrator who, when we first
sight him, is a rather sad, drab figure. We go back into his
past and see him as a boy, with a child's hopefulness and
imagination—and we discover how the hard experience
of life has turned him into the dowdy figure we re-meet at
the end. The tone is melancholy. In L.P. Hartley's *The Go
Between*—with its celebrated opening, "The past is a foreign
country: they do things differently there"—we encounter
another sad character in the present day, going with him back
into his memories of boyhood idyll and innocence to see

how he was used and deluded by grown-ups and made as he now is, disillusioned and scarred by what happened to him.

Finally, you can bookend your main story with another character: *Madame Bovary* is undoubtedly the story of Emma, but the book begins and ends with her decent if pathetic husband Charles. He is like a picture-frame, serving to heighten his wife's tragedy, and to emphasise its destructive force on someone who loved her, come what may.

Revealing the truth backwards

In some stories, the time frame seems to move in two directions at once. The information is revealed backwards: that is, each discovery takes us further back in time. Consider this scenario:

The Rose Paper

- A postman finds an old woman dead in an abandoned cottage on a big estate. He thought he knew everyone here, but has no idea who this is. In her hands the dead lady clutches a scrapbook.
- While waiting for the police, the postman takes the scrapbook from her hands. Out of the scrapbook falls a piece of rose-patterned wallpaper. But the wallpaper in the cottage is quite different.
- The postman starts asking questions. Each answer he receives sends him back to the cottage to strip away a layer of wallpaper. Beneath today's magnolia-painted woodchip he finds the rose patterned paper. Why was it covered? Beneath the rose paper he finds plain paper painted with a crude portrait of a pretty girl. Beneath the girl's portrait, he finds a stripy paper daubed with blood and the one word: *Revenge*! Beneath that, he finds a paper decorated with an 18th century coat of arms. Beneath this he finds plain paper again, with the words *Remember the crimes of 1588*! Beneath that layer he finds a concealed compartment containing a scroll of parchment, and a big iron key. But what might the key open …?

You see how the story goes ever further back.[69] At each stage, even as the postman's enquiries move forward in the present day, he (literally) peels away the layers of the past to discover an earlier motive, or a previous offence requiring revenge, or a darker secret. There's no reason to stop: you could go on discovering prior events, darker secrets, back to the dawn of history and beyond, to pagan rituals and ancient ghosts …

At each stage, the postman is not discovering *how* things happened but *why*. He is uncovering prior motivation: to mourn lost love; to conceal a rape; to take revenge; to pursue an ancient feud before that …

This digging into the past to find the truth, only to find deeper and deeper secrets, can be compelling. Notice, however, that while all the revelations are going *back* in time, the plot (the story of the postman's investigations) is moving *forward*, as the postman, in discovering the truth, faces a series of obstacles to his discovery. He overcomes each in turn and moves on to the next, and his story doubtless follows a three-act structure.

> **WORK POINT:** try constructing a plot similar to 'The Rose Paper'. Have one central conceit (like the layers of decor in a house) but have the layers covering the truth "stripped away" by different means.

Flashbacks

A story like *The Rose Paper* may employ many flashbacks. Flashbacks are often badly used, inserted because the author feels the need to explain something in the present by reference to the past. This is usually a mistake; a flashback that is not interesting in its own right should not be there. Explanation for its own sake is tedious, and should be cut. Most things don't need explaining anyway.

The Rose Paper does not have to have flashbacks; the postman could discover plenty of evidence of what happened

---

[69] An example of a building as a palimpsest—see p. 128 (above).

in the past: photographs, old diaries and letters, a grave with its headstone defaced, a sinister old painting with a puzzling detail …

The insertion of a flashback should not interrupt the structure of the story. Look (yet again) at the outline of *Casablanca*, in which one complete sequence is taken up with the extended flashback to Paris. This tells us why Rick is miserable—so, it is explanatory, but it also has great character of its own, almost a play within the play. It leads smoothly to the next development in the present-day story.

Flashbacks may, however, be designed to delay or extend the tension: Mohsin Hamid's *Reluctant Fundamentalist* is almost all flashback: the narrator's own past story creates the circumstances for the present, and also holds back the present crisis. That is, indeed, why the narrator tells his tale to a stranger in a Lahore teashop: it's a means of detaining the American visitor, keeping him there until something else can occur.

If you decide to use flashbacks, consider carefully their frequency and length. If you switch between worlds too often, there is a danger that the reader will have no time to readjust to a different set of conventions and characters, and will soon become confused. A few novels manage a frequent dislocation between past and present, but it is a difficult trick.

Sub-plots and themes

How do sub-plots fit into the sorts of structure described here and in Chapter Seven? Certainly not every novel has a sub-plot, but they are common, and the truism is that, "the main plot carries the story, but the sub-plot carries the theme". It is sometimes said that authors are more interested in their sub-plot and theme than they are in the main story.

Anna Karenina runs two stories concurrently. There is the tragic tale of Anna, her love affair with Count Vronsky, and her despairing suicide. That is the "main" story. But there is a second story (given comparable length and weight) of the landowner Levin, his wooing of Kitty, his marriage and relations with his neighbours, his brothers, and the peasants on his estate. Levin's sub-plot is much less dramatic than Anna's but it carries the theme: *How should we live in society? What is a good life?* And it is Levin's musings that end the novel—not Anna's suicide. Anna's story and Levin's overlap and touch at points in the book, but are essentially separate. They run side by side with large chunks of prose alternating, moving step by step.

William Boyd's *Restless* is a modern example. A mother is caught up in 1940s espionage, and her daughter investigates in the 1970s; the 1940s story is the main plot, but the 70s story develops the theme of mistrust and paranoia that the spy tale provokes: so, the daughter has various foreign visitors to her flat in Oxford, including an Iranian and two Germans, and she starts to mistrust them all, wondering if the Iranian is an agent of the Shah's secret police, while thinking that the Germans may be members of the Baader-Meinhof terrorist group.

Remember that a sub-plot needs its own structure, with its own acts and conclusion. But this will probably be less complex, so as not to cause confusion in the main plot.

The sub-plot may have another task: it may carry various devices or plot elements used to bring about the end of the tale. Joseph Conrad's *Victory* is set in the 19th century Dutch East Indies: an unillusioned man—Baron Heyst—retreats with his lover to a tropical island, wishing to live apart from the world. They are, inevitably, followed there from Java by murderous crooks who propose to steal whatever there is to be stolen. The final confrontation is tragic, but what actually happens in the last few pages results from tensions and rivalries that have been set up between the lesser characters, the robbers. In this way, Conrad can bring the novel to a rapid and dramatic end whenever he wants, while the broader, meditative love story of Heyst and Lena can take its course, uncluttered by too much plotting.

There is sometimes in fiction (and drama) a character called the *raisonneur*—the commentator—who helps us make sense of what we are witnessing. This person can be used to supply bits and bobs of plot fact, or may simply watch events from the shadows and offer observations to assist our understanding, or may be a secondary figure to whom our hero goes for information, comfort or advice: remember Dr Cameron in his role of elder statesman, friend, advisor and dispenser of consoling drams of whisky in the Dr Finlay stories.[70] Or they may just be someone who asks crucial questions that point our hero on their way. The *raisonneur* may inhabit a subplot, or may be self-sufficient. In Boris Pasternak's *Dr Zhivago*, the *raisonneur* is Zhivago's brother Yevgrav, a powerful policeman who gives Yuri advice and protection, but whose main purpose is to comment on Yuri's character and naivety, and the dangers building round him.[71]

Twisting multiple threads

Many novels contain multiple threads that are twisted together more or less tightly into a yarn. This may be because we are dealing with several separate stories, as in William Nicholson's *The Secret Intensity of Everyday Life* in which the stories often overlap. In other instances, such as *Anna Karenina*, the characters move in the same world and occasionally meet, but their stories have little consequence for each other. George Eliot's *Daniel Deronda* tells two stories: of an unhappy marriage among the English aristocracy, and of life among London's Jews—stories that have so little to do with each other that the critic F.R. Leavis claimed they should have been published separately.

Imagine a children's book:

Rescued by Fido

1. A group of children go out into the countryside accompanied by Fido, their faithful pooch. They find an old mine tunnel. Telling Fido to wait at the surface, they go down inside to explore.

---

[70] Based on a story by A.J. Cronin called *Country Doctor* and set in small-town Scotland in the 1920s.

[71] The figure of Yevgrav is expertly used in Robert Bolt's screenplay for the David Lean film of *Dr Zhivago*, in which Yegrav also provides bookends, as discussed above.

2. Meanwhile, up above, it starts to rain. Fido becomes uneasy.
3. Disaster underground! The rising water causes a collapse. The children are trapped.
4. Fido realises the danger, and runs back to the village police station. He barks and barks, but the police don't understand why.
5. Underground, the water level is rising …
6. The police realise that Fido wants them to follow. They set out.
7. Below ground, the situation is desperate. The water continues to rise, and the children are running out of air.
8. The police arrive with Fido. A rope is brought. Saved!

Here, two threads run in parallel: above ground and underground. You can imagine any number of additional complications and perils: maybe as the children try to climb clear of the water, one breaks a leg and cannot move! Or there could be another complete thread: maybe there are bank robbers who have hidden their loot in the mine and want to retrieve it before the police come. By switching between threads, you can:

- delay the plot by cutting away before everything is revealed,
- raise the emotional temperature, as we the audience curse the police for not hurrying back with Fido, or as we see the robbers creeping up,
- set up frequent cliff-hangers, switching to the police station just as little Billy (underground) is hanging on by his fingernails and beginning to slip,
- give an impression of complexity and texture to what is really a very simple tale.

Parallel threads may be used in different time-frames. I've mentioned Iain Pears' *An Instance of The Fingerpost* as an example of a 'Rashomon' story of multiple threads. Pears specialises in this sort of structure, sometimes spaced over a wide time span; his *Dream of Scipio* has three stories all set in the same small town in Provence and with a linking theme: one part occurs during World War Two, another during the Black Death of the 1300s, and a further part during the Dark Ages as the Roman occupation succumbs to barbarian incursions. Each section develops the themes explored in other sections, and each story is enriched by echoes of the others.

William Boyd's *Restless* employs similar time-spaced threads from the outset in the 1970s when the daughter drives into the countryside to visit her mother. The mother gives her daughter a memoir to read concerning her WW2 spying career. The novel continues with chapters from the 1940s memoir alternating with episodes from the daughter's 1970s life. The mother asks her daughter to track down the villain of the wartime story. So these two threads—1940s and 1970s—proceed in turn, step by step. At the end, the two come together, as the villain of the WW2 memoir is found in 1970s London by the daughter. The denouement is a confrontation between all three characters. By cutting between the two, information and revelation is paced out, and tension maintained by cliff-hangers at the ends of chapters, while the earlier story feeds the mistrust theme of the later. If there is an awkwardness, it is that the device of the written memoir seems a somewhat clunky contrivance for telling about the past in convenient chunks; we may wonder why the mother didn't just tell her daughter in person, over tea.

Shocks

Shocks are often very boring. Unpractised writers will give you pages of not very interesting narration, and then suddenly—bang! This doesn't work; the pages beforehand will do to the reader just what they did to the protagonist: lull them into paying no attention.

Paradoxically, a shock works much better if prepared. We need to have growing tension, suspicion of something coming but we're not sure what. Our *On The Shore* hero Gibson, for instance, is a talented but impoverished artist, now facing ruin, and he has written to a kindly millionaire aunt for help. His creditors are closing in, his children are hungry, but he loves and trusts his aunt, and waits eagerly for the reply. One morning a letter falls onto the doormat and he rushes to open it—but the aunt writes: "I am informed that you are a forger, a crook and a disgrace to the family, and you'll get not a penny from me!"

This shock has been seeded with hopes, expectation and tension. Such a shock has been "earned". It was a fair bet what sort of shock was coming: for the wretched Gibson, it was bound to be financial bad news. So the nature of the shock may be clearly signalled in advance, but still shocking. Graham Greene wrote a witty little novel called *Dr Fischer of Geneva or: The Bomb Party*. A rich industrialist plays a game with a group of six avaricious guests. He sits them down to an out-of-doors dinner and points out a bran tub nearby. In the bran tub is a cracker, one for each guest. In five of the crackers there is a cheque for two million Swiss francs; in the sixth there is a bomb; he asks them to go in turn to the tub, to take a cracker and pull it. Hesitantly, one by one, they go to the tub—but with each cracker that does *not* explode, the odds grow worse for those that are left … How strange: we are expecting to be shocked. We'd be positively cross if no shock occurred. There is, however, a twist: we've been set up for a particular shocking event—but that is not quite what happens.

For a true-life version, consider the bomb plot to kill Hitler. Colonel Claus von Stauffenberg carries a bomb in a suitcase into the concrete bunker where Hitler is meeting with his staff. He places it under the table. The detonator is ticking. He must find an excuse for leaving the room. He exits … and there is a colossal explosion behind him. In one sense, this is no shock at all, since we know that Hitler did not die that day. It is, nonetheless, shocking.

A shock can be quite unpredictable, although carefully prepared. Michel Faber's early short story *Some Rain Must Fall* is set in a Scottish primary school where a new teacher has arrived. This teacher has specialist skills, and has been brought in to deal with a difficult problem. We are not sure what the problem is, but we see that the children are feeling very vulnerable and fragile. The teacher's job is to help them cope with something terrible that has happened. At the end, one of the children reveals what that was—and it is deeply shocking.

If well set-up, something quite slight can be remarkably shocking. I have already mentioned (p. 144) the moment in *Sophie's Choice* where beautiful young Sophie is glimpsed in the mirror looking ghastly because she is not wearing her dentures. In another book this might be a comic moment; in William Styron's novel it is devastating, because we have been carefully prepared: we know that Sophie is lovely, but we also know that her admirer feels vaguely that she is "doomed". We know that she is sexy, but we also know that she is a survivor of Auschwitz. And there have been unsettling mentions of suicide … Now we are given a sudden image of Sophie looking like a death mask—and all those carefully pre-prepared elements come crashing in upon us.

Shocks do not have to be distressing and negative. In John Fowles's *The French Lieutenant's Woman*, there is one episode of sex. It happens suddenly and dramatically, sweeping those concerned off their feet; as one reviewer wrote: "The sex, when it comes, blows your head off." But this has been carefully prepared; for a couple of hundred pages, the sexual tension has been growing between these two characters. We know that they are powerfully attracted but also that the man is engaged to another woman; we know that this should not happen … The shock, once again, is earned.

Foreshadowing

Many aspects of a plot need preparation. To get the most from an emotional or moral climax, even in a gentle, thoughtful tale, one should prepare the ground with clues and hints, seeding and foreshadowing. Thus, when the reader reaches the moment of crisis, alarm bells will ring: they will understand that they have arrived at a crucial moment.

The Door is a strange novel by Magda Szabó[72] concerning the intense relationship between a young Hungarian woman

---

[72] Magda Szabó is a Hungarian novelist little known in English but celebrated elsewhere in Europe, the winner of many French and Hungarian prizes. *The Door* was written in her seventies. It is available in an English language paperback.

and her unusual housekeeper, Emerence. The climax of the novel comes when Emerence is ill, and her employer brings help to force open her front door—an act seen by Emerence as a gross betrayal. Everything builds towards this, and the set-ups begin with the book's title, *The Door*, followed by a first chapter—called 'The Door'—in which the young author dreams of trying to force open an impenetrable door. In synopsis this sounds crude, but the effect is remarkable.

Foreshadowing also makes clear to the reader what sort of story they are embarked upon. My own Tibetan novel *Blue Poppies* begins with this sentence:

> Before the Chinese burned Jyeko village, a tax official from Lhasa stayed there.

The actual burning of the village—a pivotal moment—does not occur until half way through the book.

Orhan Pamuk's *Museum of Innocence* climaxes in a tragic car crash. This is carefully prepared throughout the novel; the car is virtually a character in the story, and is even there on the English-language hardback's wrapper. There are frequent references to dangerous driving, and driving while drunk. A second set-up concerns a pretty butterfly earring, worn by the heroine and admired by the hero, often mislaid and puzzled over in the course of the book, and now suddenly there on her ear as the two main characters at last set out in the car. Two foreshadowed elements have come together …

Sophie's Choice has plenty of foreshadowing. Sophie has survived Auschwitz, but at a terrible moral cost; she is now (1947) living in Brooklyn, New York. The young American narrator, Stingo, is infatuated with Sophie. Before he even meets her, however, Stingo's father sends him a newspaper cutting, reporting that another girl whom he adored in his teens has inexplicably committed suicide. Stingo then meets the even more lovely Sophie. He has hardly known her for twenty-four hours before he concludes that she is somehow fated. The reader can (as Americans might say) "do the math".

In a complex plot, make sure that you prepare such key elements well. The reader may not even know that they are picking up important hints—but when they come to the crucial moment, they will know.

WORK POINT: look again at novels that you know well. Identify any foreshadowing that takes place. In any new novel that you read, look out for this.

Summary points

- Before you can work out a plot, you must know what the book is actually *about*. What is the heart of the story you are trying to tell? What is the question?
- A plot is a mystery. Plotting is the business of establishing what the mystery is, and deciding how the truth will be discovered.
- The complexity of any plot is your decision. You could have everything revealed in one letter, or you could make your hero work for every scrap.
- As information is revealed, it should create further questions for the next sequence of the story.
- Too much plot complexity will make it difficult to explore character.
- Resist using flashbacks for explanation as far as possible. Do things really need explaining?
- Consider carefully how sub-plots and parallel threads in the story will be intertwined.
- Shocks usually need set-up and preparation.
- Foreshadowing will help the reader to understand key moments, and will add to the richness of the reading experience.

13 Dialogue

Many new writers are nervous of dialogue; they fear that they cannot make it realistic. Students' dialogue does tend to be long-winded or redundant—there's often just too much of it. But realism is not usually the point. Dialogue is one of the tools of story-telling. It has various tasks: to reveal character, and the different status of characters; to advance the story; to enliven and humanise the scenes, often with humour; and to make plot information interesting. These are all things that we actually do when we talk: we try to display our character, assert our status, enliven social occasions, and interest listeners in what we are saying. But in fiction, you will have to do it much more efficiently.

Firstly, consider who is talking to whom, and the appropriate differences in register.

Register

"Register" means the level of correctness and formality of speech. In any dialogue, our register will vary, sometimes subtly, sometimes grossly. It will be affected not just by who we are, but also by whom we are talking *to*. Speakers of English often make a simple mistake in (for example) French, using the familiar "tu" in addressing someone they have just met, when they should be using the more formal "vous"—which is an error of register. Our register will depend on whether we wish to seem sympathetic, or to keep our distance. Do we hope to identify with a group, or to mark ourselves out? Do we need to be respectful—to our elders or seniors perhaps—or are we being familiar with children, friends or lovers? Are we being seductive or insulting? Do we want to reveal the truth, or to hide it? Do we need to take on a specialist vocabulary? Are we affecting a professional tone with regard to something we know nothing about—bluffing, in fact? Are we impatient to be gone, or wanting to settle in for a chat? Are we being purposefully humble, or unpleasantly condescending? It comes down to that fundamental question: *What is it, at this moment, that my character wants?*

I mentioned in Chapter Eleven *The Tailor of Panama*, John le Carré's story of Pendel, a working-class criminal from London who sets himself up in Central America as a high class Savile Row gentleman's outfitter. When a new, well-heeled customer called Mr Osnard appears, Pendel's speech is a mix of the obsequious and the confiding: 'I see you favour brown … It becomes you very well, if I may say so, brown.' While chattering, Mr Pendel appears to be always casting doubt on his own understanding: 'Your average Panamanian gentleman seems to consider brown unmanly, I don't know why.' And again: 'I always say it's the too-much-red that spoils a good brown, I don't know if I'm right.' The calculated self-denigration is humble but at the same moment calculated to solicit the response: I'm sure you *are* right, Mr Pendel. No one understands these things better.

Remember the opening of *Wuthering Heights* (see page 36). The pompous Mr Lockwood reports his first meeting with Heathcliff:

> I announced my name.
> 'Mr Heathcliff?' I said.
> A nod was the answer.
> 'Mr Lockwood your new tenant, sir. I do myself the honour of calling as soon as possible, after my arrival, to express the hope that I have not inconvenienced you by my perseverance in soliciting the occupation of Thrushcross Grange: I heard, yesterday, you had some thoughts …'
> 'Thrushcross Grange is my own, sir,' he interrupted me, wincing. 'I should not allow anyone to inconvenience me if I could hinder it—walk in!'
> The "walk in" was uttered with closed teeth and expressed the sentiment, "Go to the Deuce!"

Lockwood enjoys the contrast between his formality and Heathcliff's surliness, but doesn't realise that it is his own contortions which sound ridiculous.

Michel Faber's *The Crimson Petal & The White* is a portrait of the lives of Victorian prostitutes, and of the wealthy household into which one these trollops (the heroine, Sugar) worms her way. Here, the master of the house creeps up behind two women—one his wife Agnes, one his maidservant—in an unusual situation:

> For there, side by side on the stone floor, are Agnes and the scullery-maid Janey, both with their backs to him and their arses in the air, crawling along on their hands and knees, dipping scrubbing brushes by turns into a large pail of soapy water. And conversing while they're at it ...
>
> 'Well, ma'am,' Janey is saying. 'I *tries* to wash every dish the same, but the fing is, you don't expeck *fingerbowls* to be all that dirty, do yer?'
>
> 'No, no, of course not,' pants Agnes as she scrubs.
>
> 'Well, neiver did I,' rejoins the girl. 'Neiver did I. And so there I was, with Cook shoutin' and bawlin' at me, and wavin' these fingerbowls at me, and I carn't deny as they 'ad a cake o'grease all under them, but honest to crikey, ma'am, it was fingerbowls, and Cook must know they's normally so clean ...'
>
> 'Yes, yes,' sympathises the mistress. 'You poor girl.'
>
> 'And this ... This 'ere's blood.'

Janey's low-register prattle is conveyed by spelling, punctuation and speech patterns. The comedy comes from the contrast with the polite mistress of the house, by the absurdity of the posture, and by the incongruity of Agnes being there at all. Playing with register like this performs many of the tasks for dialogue: providing humour, plot information, and mood, as well as characterisation.

Various formal registers will typify different professions— as in the psychiatric case history appended to Ian McEwan's *Enduring Love*, which sounded sufficiently like a doctor writing to fool my doctor wife. A student once showed me an economics essay in which she had repeatedly referred to "individuals functioning in the commercial environment". When I remarked that she could have written "people shopping", she objected: "But I have to sound like an economist!" The writer of fiction has to be able to make people sound like economists, where required.

> **WORK POINT:** re-write the following dialogue.

Here is a moment of dialogue between a doctor and a personnel (HR) officer at a hospital. The doctor is newly arrived and needs accommodation. Try reading these lines aloud with varying status expressed by your voice. In one version, make the doctor very senior, arrogant and overbearing, with the personnel officer timid; in a second reading, reverse the status so that the doctor is a newly qualified junior cowed by a bullying functionary.

Then: re-write the dialogue as prose. How could you do this effectively but economically, to make the point of status? What changes might you make to the speech, to reflect the personal differences? What actions or descriptions might you add in to help?

Doctor	May I come in?
HR	Please do. And who are you?
Doctor	Jenkyns. Dr Julian Jenkyns. I've come about the accomodation.
HR	Oh, have you?
Doctor	I shall be here for six months.
HR	And …?
Doctor	You've given me one small room.
HR	And what were you expecting?

Conveying accent and speech types

Throughout *The Crimson Petal & The White*, Michel Faber's rendition of speech is skilfully varied; in such a long novel, even with a fast-moving story, many readers would find only non-stop low-register dialogue rather wearisome.

Some writers, however, specialise in a densely consistent evocation of registers, accents, or of the English of foreign-language speakers. Two Scottish examples are James Kelman, with his renditions of drunken down-and-out Glaswegians, and Irvine Welsh with his low-life Leith (from the old port area of Edinburgh). This does not make for easy reading: I used to live in Leith myself, but I cannot always understand this Scots or Scottish English (Irvine Welsh uses both, as spoken by different characters within the one novel). Often the trick for the reader is to start by reading out loud; after a while one tunes in. Kelman and Welsh are appealing to particular markets and particular reader sympathies; other readers may be turned off.

Several of my students have written in strong accents or dialect; they have sometimes included a glossary. This rarely works; few things are more irritating for a reader than to have to stop and look something up. If you *don't* give a glossary, the reader will just guess and (if you don't overwhelm them) will usually guess right from the context. There may be more common vocabulary that will work as well: why call something a "forbytuttle" if you can equally well call it an axe? On the other hand, for a bit of colour, the deft placing of such local vocabulary works if the context makes things clear, as in: "She crept up behind him with a good sharp forbytuttle and split his head open." Meanwhile, the insertion of the occasional foreign expletive can be effective. Nicolas Freeling's Amsterdammers will once in a while lob in a Dutch or French oath—"Je les emmerde!"—but a little goes a long way.

Conveying voices or accents with punctuation—as Michel Faber does—is fine in short spurts, but will become tiresome if continued for long. The other approach is to listen for speech patterns, rhythms and catch-phrases. In *The Tailor of Panama*, Le Carré captures the tone of Andy Osnard, an overbearing product of minor English boarding schools, with a speech mannerism: "Hell …" (as in: "Who the hell is …?" or "What the hell are you …?"). If Andy wishes to know someone's name, he says: "Hell's he?" If he is puzzled by a request, he'll say: "Hell for?"

So a tiny tag readily characterises his speech and his personality. This can be true of a whole society: in the work of the Nigerian novelist Chinua Achebe, such as *Things Fall Apart,* we meet strikingly different speech in which conversations seem to consist largely of vivid Ibo proverbs. Look for those characteristic patterns—but beware of cliché: don't have Welshmen say "look you!" at the end of every sentence.

Conveying information

In some dialogue, conveying information may be a higher priority than characterisation. However, you must not lose sight of character. Here is a conversation from Conan Doyle's *The Hound of The Baskervilles,* in which Sherlock Holmes has visitors:

> Dr Mortimer started violently. 'Followed! By whom?'
> 'That, unfortunately, is what I cannot tell you. Have you among your neighbours or acquaintances on Dartmoor any man with a full, black beard?'
> 'No—or, let me see—why, yes, Barrymore, Sir Charles's butler, is a man with a full, black beard.'
> 'Ha! Where is Barrymore?'
> 'He is in charge of the Hall.'
> 'We had best ascertain if he is really there, or if by any possibility he might be in London.'
> 'How can you do that?'
> 'Give me a telegraph form. "Is all ready for Sir Henry?" That will do. Address to Mr Barrymore, Baskerville Hall. Which is the nearest telegraph office? Grimpen. Very good, we will send a second wire to the postmaster, Grimpen …'

This is very efficient dialogue. A great deal of information is conveyed, but at the same time character is developed, indications for the future plot are given, and the mood is sustained. We see how Holmes takes charge of the situation, asking his incisive questions, giving clear instructions, while no one (not even a doctor) presumes to interrupt him or to speak unless spoken to. The dialogue is very swift, and though there is not a single "Holmes said", we have little doubt who is speaking.

Notice also that characters do not use each other's names: there is no repetition of, "Well, Doctor" or "I see, Mr Holmes." Again, these occur only sparingly in Conan Doyle—and in reality, people seldom use each other's names in conversation unless they are needing to attract attention. It is often the mark of poor dialogue, that people name each other too much. It suggests that the writer does not have the conversation under control, and fears that the reader will be confused if names are not scattered about.

However, the *Baskerville* dialogue is hardly realistic; Holmes requests information as he writes the telegram, but we don't hear anyone give it to him. A shorthand is being used.

All dialogue is artificial

Here, for comparison, is a passage from one of Ian Rankin's Rebus novels, *The Falls*. The Rebus books contain a great deal of dialogue, some of it propelling the plot, some for mood and atmosphere. This is a late-night conversation between two of Rebus's colleagues: Grant (in the street downstairs) and Siobhan, who wants to go to bed:

'Hello?' She slumped on the sofa, phone to her ear.
'Siobhan? It's Grant.'
'Where are you?'
'I've just been ringing your doorbell.'
'Mustn't be working. What can I do for you?'
'Letting me in would be a start.'
'I'm tired, Grant. Just going to bed.'
'Five minutes, Siobhan.'
'I don't think so.'
'Oh'. The silence was like a third party, some huge, humourless friend only one of them had invited.
'Just go home, eh? I'll see you in the morning.'
'That might be too late for the Quizmaster.'

'Oh, you're here to talk about work?' She slid her free hand up her body, tucking it under the arm holding the phone.

'Not exactly,' he admitted.

This is apparently much more "natural", especially in its short sentences; even so, a number of devices are being used: for a start, the broken doorbell. The pace is varied by describing one pause ("the silence …") and by inserting a physical action (the movement of Siobhan's hand) which gives a second pause. We are given names four times; we are given indications of tone ("her voice hardening"); and we are told what is meant by speeches ("he admitted"). Very little plot information is given, only a passing indication of work tomorrow. This dialogue is all about a relationship. It has a particular task to perform, and it is just as contrived as Conan Doyle's.

As it must be. If you eavesdrop on real conversations, whether among your friends and colleagues or between strangers on a train, you will appreciate that entirely "natural" dialogue would be of little use in a novel: it rambles, it stutters and starts, it hesitates, it gets into tiny knots and tangles that have to be sorted out. Try transcribing such dialogue and you will see that it is pretty tedious to read.

As with every other aspect of your novel: dialogue must work for you. Decide what it is you need to achieve, and design your conversations accordingly. Above all, never bore your readers. When you know what the passage needs to accomplish, you will almost certainly be able to cut much of it.

> **WORK POINT:** pull some novels off the shelf: how much dialogue is there? What explains the differences—is the information or mood conveyed in other ways? Take any one conversation: what is the author requiring it to do, at this moment in the story? How natural is it, really? What devices are used? How well does it work?

Lessons from film dialogue

Film dialogue is by no means always better than fiction; however, film has several lessons to teach. Film writers have to be economical. They cannot waffle, because that would mean several million dollars-worth of extra screen time. They have to keep the story moving, or audiences will be bored and the film will lose money. Producers and directors will be breathing down their necks to ensure these things, while editors will cut anything redundant. Meanwhile, if the characterisation is rubbish, or stilted, then the actors will protest, as will the critics.

So it is worth examining screen dialogue. Scores of scripts are available online at various sites,[73] where you will find most of the English language films that you have seen of late. You will see how economical and deft a professional script can be. Major jumps in story can be made in a few words: "showing" triumphs over "telling".

But you may also decide that the characterisation seems rather thin—that film dialogue can seem, in fact, somewhat characterless. This is because a screenwriter relies on actors to bring speech to life. Deborah Moggach—who is both a best-selling novelist and an experienced screenwriter—described this difference in the journal of the Society of Authors, in particular her experience of adapting Jane Austen's *Pride & Prejudice* for the screen. Where Austen gives her characters supple, individualised dialogue, Moggach's script reads: "I'm here on holiday with my uncle and aunt." "Are you having a pleasant trip?"—which, as Moggach herself says, is utterly banal—but the actors' faces and manner will convey all the emotion and nuance on screen that the novelist must provide in other ways.

> **WORK POINT:** select two or three scripts online. Take a page of dialogue from each and consider carefully what it is intended to achieve: is it a matter of story information? Characterisation? Mystery and questioning—or all of these? Try re-writing it, rendering it as prose fiction. How well does it work? Could you convert it to reported speech? What might you need to add or alter to make this good fiction writing?

---

[73] For instance, www.dailyscript.com and the 'Writersroom' on the BBC website.

Summary points

- All dialogue in fiction is artificial. It has particular tasks to achieve, particular information to convey. Decide first what the conversation needs to accomplish.
- Consider register, or degree of formality. What does your character intend by their speech, and how formal must they be to achieve it? At this moment: what does your character want?
- Use a contrast of low and high register to indicate relative status, and for enlivening effect.
- Use register for professional status also. Reading professional journals will help you to catch the tone.
- Accent and dialect can be conveyed by punctuation and by characteristic speech patterns. But don't weary your reader with endless peculiar spellings or glossaries.
- Use interruptions and physical moves to vary the pace.
- Look at film scripts for lessons in dialogue economy.

14 Fiction and film

I've cited many films in this guide as examples and comparisons, for instance as regards dialogue. This emphasis is partly because I love the cinema, partly because I was trained as a screen writer, but also because the overlap between the two forms is so great, and not only in the reliance of both on three-act narrative structure. These are the two principal forms of story-telling today; they have enormous influence on each other, and each holds lessons for the other.

Books for Hollywood

A friend tells me that he rarely reads new novels, preferring the classics, because, "new novels are just film scripts in disguise: lots of action, a bit of description and character, but little else." He feels that such books betray the fundamental strength of fiction: a level of pyschological subtlety and penetration that film cannot match.

Techniques in fiction and drama are different. But have the forms now become confused? How far is the writing of modern novels influenced by film? One hears that such-and-such a book would make a great film; was it perhaps designed to be filmed? Was that (and a fat optioning fee) the whole object? Is that how you—the novelist—should be thinking and writing?

It is undeniable that some stories read like films. One recent prize-winning novel tells of a group of foreign soldiers caught up in another country's civil war. They are, at last, surrounded by national troops in a small town, and the final battle ensues. The cast includes a tragic hero, a strong-willed and sensual woman, an intellectual trying to see a way out of the situation, and two villains, one a violent thug and one much more sinister and psychopathic. In the conclusion, everything seems calculated for the last ten minutes of a movie. The tragic hero kills the thug—but is himself slain.

The woman and the thinker might leave together—but it cannot be. The foreign band-of-brothers depart after handshakes all round and with their heads held high. The sinister psychopath flees—and we almost hear him cry, "The world shall hear from me again!" The final chapter of this otherwise most original story reads like *Star Wars* crossed with *The Magnificent Seven*.

It may be argued that such an ending is satisfying; everyone gets what's coming to them. The various plots are concluded, and storytelling-justice has prevailed. In certain genres (notably crime and romance), a fully concluded story is expected by the market, and the author cannot be blamed for complying. But in general fiction, something more open-ended, suggestive and stimulating is possible. If a novelist structures a book as though it were a film in the hope that it will be optioned, they will do everyone a disservice.

Perhaps three-quarters of Oscar-winning films are adaptations from books, from *Gone With The Wind* to *The English Patient* and beyond. A closer look reveals, however, that many successful adaptations are taken from rather difficult texts. Michael Ondaatje's *The English Patient* is a complex, rather rambling novel; the screenwriter Anthony Minghella performed heroic surgery to fashion a film out of it. The same goes for *L.A. Confidential*, where the convoluted plot of James Ellroy's book is barely recognisable: it reportedly took seven drafts of the film script to extract a workable story from the novel; the writer and director were drawn to the characters, not the plot. Robert Altman's film *Short Cuts* was assembled from a collection of Raymond Carver stories, and moved from the stories' original Pacific North-West location to Los Angeles. A few novels written to be filmed have succeeded. Graham Greene's *The Third Man*[74] is perhaps the best known example: Greene began work on his screenplay by writing a novella, to get a fuller sense of the story. After the film was released, he re-worked the novella and published it. But such successes are rare. Writing your book as if it were half-way to being a film is a waste of time.

---

[74] 1950. Filmed by Carol Reed in 1949 with Joseph Cotton and Orson Wells.

On the other hand, novelists can learn a great deal from film—which, after all, has been with us for a century now, and is a highly developed form. Comparisons between film and fiction highlight aspects of the novel that you perhaps suspected, but may not have thought about in detail. We've already looked at dialogue; what about the visuals?

Camerawork: What are you looking at?

A fundamental skill in film-making—of which the screen-writer must be as conscious as the director—is an awareness of what you are looking at. This is an important lesson for the fiction writer. It is vital not to cut about to the extent that the reader becomes confused and the narrative direction weakened. In a well-directed film, the camera shots have a narrative logic; they tell the story. This holds true for novels. As you write your fiction, consider what you are asking your reader to look at in the mind's eye, and have it make visual sense. Cinema's terms of reference can help.

A very old example: Chaucer's *Troilus & Criseyde* has the young Prince Troilus trying to win the love of Criseyde. Her uncle Pandare goes to her private rooms and speaks glowingly about Troilus: just the noble protector she needs, a paragon among men. Then there is a commotion outside: Troilus is coming, riding along the street that leads towards Criseyde's house. He is just back from the day's battle, weary but heroic. Criseyde goes to the window overlooking the street and watches the warrior approaching. We move from a close interior to a long shot. Criseyde observes Troilus ride all along the street towards her, coming into close-up—and in an exquisite moment, she feels the sudden intoxication of love as powerfully as if she'd swallowed a large glass of cognac:

> Criseyde let all his looks sink
> softly into her heart, and
> sighed: Who gave me this drink?[75]

---

[75] *Troilus and Criseyde* Book Two, ll. 649–651. Originally: "Criseyde gan al his chere aspien/and leet it so softe in hire herte synke/that to hireself she seyde, "Who yaf me drynke?"

Never mind that this was written *circa* 1385; it is a truly cinematic moment.

It is such a lovely moment that I couldn't resist borrowing it for my own novel *Blue Poppies*, set in Tibet in 1949. The Greeks are now Chinese, Criseyde is now a crippled Tibetan woman called Puton, her uncle is now a monk called Khenpo Nima, and Troilus is now a young Scottish radio technician working in Tibet. Otherwise, nothing has changed since 1385. It begins in Puton's room overlooking the village street:

> 'Come here. Now you shall see.' Khenpo Nima interrupted her so abruptly that she was startled. She fumbled for her stick. He called impatiently, 'Come to the window. Let me help … Quick, now!'
>
> As he carried Puton to the small window, a rider came into full view in the lane. Jamie rode with a light touch, letting the pony find its own pace, picking its way through the rubbish and the bones. He wore a small knapsack on his shoulder, with his hat off to catch the last sun. The breeze tousled his hair, he was fit and gentle, nodding and smiling to walkers in the lane … Puton drank in his look, saying not a word.
>
> 'There's an end to your danger,' laughed Khenpo Nima … He returned her to the bed in one effortless lift. For a moment, Puton felt herself flying.

An interior close shot moving to an exterior long shot, and back again. In fact, *Blue Poppies* began life as a film script, commissioned by a London producer and written while I was working at a Los Angeles film school.

Fiction often uses the panoramic shot, sometimes to begin a story: the classic examples of Conrad's *Nostromo* and Thomas Hardy's *Return of the Native* were discussed in Chapter Nine. Here is another opening, and another rider coming towards us, from perhaps the most famous of all cowboy novels, Jack Schaefer's *Shane*:

> He rode into our valley in the summer of '89. I was a kid then, barely topping the backboard of father's

old chuck-wagon. I was on the upper rail of our small corral, soaking up the summer sun, when I saw him far down the road where it swung into the valley from the open plain beyond.

In that clear Wyoming air I could see him plainly, though he was still several miles away. There seemed nothing remarkable about him, just another stray horseman riding up the road towards the cluster of frame buildings that was our town. Then I saw a pair of cowhands, loping past him, stop and stare after him with a curious intentness.

He came steadily on, straight through the town without slackening pace, until he reached the fork a half-mile below our place. One branch turned left across the river ford and on to Luke Fletcher's big spread. The other bore ahead along the right bank where we homesteaders had pegged our claims in a row along the valley. He hesitated briefly, studying the choice, and moved steadily again on our side.

As he came near, what impressed me first were his clothes …

This is pure cinema, in the sense that everything is expressed in vision and movement. There is an emphasis on clarity of view (the farmhands, too, turn to stare). There is a measured pace both in Shane's riding and in the prose, and the steady drawing near-to-camera, from several miles away to close enough that we can study his clothes. His steady coming epitomises the way in which he enters and fills the lives of the people. Shane seems imbued with moral force, passing by the rich man's ranch and opting instead for the company of the simple people, the homesteaders: as so often in good storytelling, we have that resonant moment of choice, seen here in a long shot. This choice—and Shane's loyalty to the farmers who welcome him—drives the story.

These three examples are all positive in tone. The opposite may be the case. My third novel, *Glenfarron*, is partly set in a house in the Scottish Highlands. This house contains a *camera obscura*, an old-fashioned optical contrivance of lenses and mirrors that enables one to project an image of the outside world onto a round, white table.[76]

The novel contains a ghost story: the central character, Anna, is able to see through the *camera obscura* a figure long dead:

> She turned the lens further, skimming over cottages and byres. As she completed the circle, bringing the view back to the pub, she depressed the angle and brought the view closer, until she was looking down at the kirk. And there he stood, looking up at her. He stood out, stark against the white field of the kirkyard, the severe lines of his cape making an unmistakeable geometry, his long staff a harsh black vertical stroke. He was waiting, and looking up at Anna.
>
> She lowered her hands slowly, as though fearing to provoke him with sudden movement.
>
> They stared at each other for an eternity, both immobile. Anna stopped breathing. Then he stirred; at once, her hands flew back to the control rods. She pulled and manipulated, keeping the figure in view as he walked across the kirkyard past the stunted yew. She was unpractised, she was unskilful, and as he came through the gateway into the lane she lost him, and gave a little gasp of fear. With tweakings and twists she found him once more, moving up the driveway towards the house. He was striding briskly. Frantically she sidled round the white table top, swinging the optics to keep track of him as he approached. He passed behind a stand of trees, and panic seized her as he failed to reappear and she thought she'd lost him again—but he was only now coming out from behind the trees, there he was! Still coming, still gazing up at her, so brightly illuminated that she believed she could see the black of his eyes seeking her out.
>
> Then he was into the yard, and the optics would not depress further. He was lost to view, he was too close …

---

[76] There are a few of these devices in Britain, including one in Edinburgh by the castle, one in Dumfries, and one at Portmerion in North Wales.

Anna is the unskilled cameraman. This device of viewing a ghostly figure through a (more modern) surveillance system occurs also in Catherine O'Flynn's *What Was Lost*, set in that hellish shopping mall. The security guards keep seeing on their screens a little girl who seems lost. At last they spot her in a part of the mall where it will be easy for one of them—Scott—to intercept her. His colleague Kurt watches the encounter on a monitor:

> Kurt adjusted the angle of the camera a tiny amount, so that the mirrored door from which Scott would emerge was visible in the corner of the screen with the girl ... The door opened slowly and Scott emerged directly in front of the girl ... Scott seemed hesitant. He edged a couple of steps towards her and then stopped. Kurt watched him raise his radio to his mouth ...
>
> 'Kurt, give me some more instructions.'
> 'Just speak to her, what else can I say?'
> 'Where is she? I mean, which way did she go?'
> 'Are you blind? She's standing in front of you.'
> ... But Scott didn't talk to the girl. Instead he turned around slowly, as if he was too scared to move fast, tilted his head up towards the camera and said, 'There's nobody here, mate.'

These are obviously cinematic moments, literally viewed through a camera. For a rather different but also painful episode that derives from cinema, you may like to turn again to the passage from *Blue Poppies* where the Tibetan villagers look back from the mountain pass at their own village.[77]

The novel's "camera" may take the audience through "the set" to introduce them to some new world—a world that could be nightmarish. Michel Faber, in the opening of *The Crimson Petal & The White* has the narrator drawing the reader through the grim backstreets of Victorian London. Notice the present tense. The *fiction* is that the narrator is a pimp and the reader is perhaps looking for a prostitute; the *technique*, however, is that of the camera leading the viewer:

---

[77] See p. 105–6 above.

When I first caught your eye and you decided to come with me, you were probably thinking you would simply arrive and make yourself at home. Now that you're actually here, the air is bitterly cold, and you find yourself being led along in complete darkness, stumbling on uneven ground, recognising nothing … You were hoping I would … at least show you a good time. Now you hesitate, still holding onto me, but tempted to let me go …. You blunder forward into the haze of your own spent breath, still following me. The cobblestones beneath your feet are wet and mucky, the air is frigid and smells of sour spirits and slowly dissolving dung …

The main characters in this story, with whom you want to become intimate, are nowhere near here … You may wonder, then, why did I bring you here? … Watch your step on these stairs; some of them are rotten …

Be alert and precise about what you see in your imagination, and what you want your reader to see. As you write, take hold of the mental image that you have, and consider: what can I see just now? What angle am I viewing it from? What can I perhaps *not* see? Do my characters share my point of view?

This is not a skill that derives from cinema; it is very much older than that. Remember the moment in Henry James's *The Portrait of A Lady*[78] in which Isabel Archer glimpses the truth about her marriage even as she glimpses her husband and Madame Merle though a doorway:

Just beyond the threshold of the drawing-room she stopped short, the reason for her doing so being that she had received an impression. The impression had, in strictness, nothing unprecedented; but she felt it as something new, and the soundlessness of her step gave her time to take in the scene before she interrupted it.

What she sees is a mystery and a truth, framed by the doorway: a "still". Chaucer's Troilus, thinking about his

---

[78] *The Portrait of a Lady* (1881), Chapter 40. See the discussion on p. 91 above.

lovely Criseyde, projects an image of her within his own mental *camera obscura*. Chaucer writes:

> Thus he came to make a mirror of his mind
> In which he saw her all complete before him.[79]

So: not new. However, the language of cinema that we are all so familiar with, of visualisation and camera angles, is a useful way to deal with this aspect of writing, and it teaches many lessons—above all, the importance of *seeing your story*.

Authors of film and fiction

A good number of novelists have also worked in film: Raymond Chandler and Graham Greene are only two of the best-known examples of novelists-cum-screenwriters. Among contemporaries there is William Nicholson who is well established as a novelist for children (*The Wind Singer* series) and for adults (*The Secret Intensity of Everyday Life*), who is also a leading screenwriter (*Shadowlands, Gladiator*) and who has on occasion directed from his own screenplay (*Firelight*).

However, this sort of cross-career sometimes fails in ways that illustrate differences between film and fiction. Just before the outbreak of World War 2, a number of European writers headed for the freedom of the USA; some, under a special programme, were given work in the film industry. One exile was Thomas Mann, the Nobel-winning German author of profound and very long novels such as *Buddenbrooks* and *The Magic Mountain*. Mann was entranced by the movie industry and tried his hand at scripts; it didn't suit his writing style at all. There is a story that Mann was asked to write scenes depicting a fictional marriage in trouble; Mann came up with page after page of laborious analysis. These were shown to a Hollywood hack screenwriter who threw up his hands: No, no, that's not the way. Look, said the hack: you set the scene in a hotel lobby; a lift is coming down; as the

---

[79] *Troilus and Criseyde* Book One ll. 365–6. Originally: "Thus gan he make a mirour of his mynde/ in which he saugh al holly hire figure."

doors open, a middle-aged couple step out of the lift, but the husband only has eyes for a beautiful girl who is standing there—until his angry wife yanks him away. There you are: a marriage in trouble.

That is "show, don't tell" in action. Thomas Mann made a hopeless screenwriter, though as a profound, enquiring novelist of the human condition—frequently telling, often with minimal showing—he has seldom been bettered.[80]

---

[80] Henry James is another example; he badly wanted to be a playwright, and was only put off this career by the failure of his play *Guy Domville* in London. Nonetheless, critics have sometimes noted that James has a dramatist's instincts for structure and scene building.

Summary points

- Be prepared to learn from film, but be alert to the differences between film and fiction, especially as regards "showing and telling".
- Don't set out to write a novel to be filmed. It won't happen.
- Train yourself to see your story as you tell it, and thus bring your reader to see it with you.

15 **Short stories**

Why bother?

Why bother with short stories at all? In the UK at least, although there is some small market in magazines, it is not easy to get story collections published, and editions are likely to be tiny.[81] There is a perception in Britain that nobody buys stories, and few publishers will take the risk (in the USA the situation is a little better.) So the short story is often regarded as an orphan if not a dying art.

It is possible, however, that the story may see a renaissance with many now being published on the internet for all to see. Among authors, stories are generally held in high esteem, on a par with poetry. "I love the swift leap of a good story," wrote Raymond Carver,[82] "the excitement that often commences in the first sentence." Carver quoted the English master story-writer, V.S. Pritchett, defining the short story as "something glimpsed from the corner of the eye, in passing." Frank Kermode praised Carver in turn for his ability to encapsulate "a whole culture and a whole moral condition [in] the most seemingly slight sketch."

Many story authors draw our attention to a particular world: think of the colonial Asia depicted in the tales of W. Somerset Maugham; or the lives of American blue-collar workers explored by Carver's vignettes; or the rusty and dystopian places in J.G. Ballard's science fiction; or the quirky and eccentric folk of the Wyoming stories of Annie Proulx; or the difficult and tense existence of white farmers in the South African tales of Doris Lessing—and many

---

[81] I've been told that the average print run for a UK collection of stories is 800 copies.

[82] In the Author's Foreword reprinted in *Where I'm Calling From: Selected Stories* (1988).

others. Douglas Dunn has remarked[83] that this is a particular trait of the story: "Short stories are drawn to underdogs, life's exceptions, localities off the beaten track," and to "under-expressed, under-described lives".

Some guiding principles

I will suggest ten guiding principles for writing short stories. You will possibly disagree with several—or at least, you will be able to find counter-examples. Still, there can be a discussion.

1. Agility. In *The Pine Oil Writers' Conference* by Tim Gautreaux,[84] a character remarks: 'A story is like an airplane; you get the damned thing off the ground as soon as you can.' In a novel you may have the leisure for a landscape or character description to begin with; in a story you don't. Launch straight in. The process of evoking the world and characters must happen along with an immediate engagement with the events.

2. Come in late, and leave early. An invaluable mantra, originally coined for dramatists regarding scene construction, but equally applicable to the short story. Enter the narrative as late in events as possible, and finish quickly.

3. Intensity. Every word in every sentence must count, must be working for the story, more so than in a novel. This is not just a matter of getting everything in under a 2,500 word competition limit, or the tighter constraints of an internet site. It is to do with the *experience* of the story: a single, intense moment of fiction.

4. Accuracy. You cannot make a broad statement and then qualify it later. Say things once, and say them right first time.

5. A single focus. Keep to one strongly defined voice, one point of view. In general, short stories do not have a subplot,

---

[83] In his introduction to *The Oxford Book of Scottish Short Stories* (1995).
[84] In his 2010 story collection *Waiting For The Evening News.*

or not much of one. You should be taking a single experience and exploring it as far as you can. It is not impossible to weave different narrative threads together, but you run the danger of leaving each one thin and unconvincing, and of confusing the reader who wants to know: what is this about?—and who has little time to discover the answer.

6. Light structure. Some stories suffer from a heavy-handed imposition of structure: there before us we see the beginning, the middle and the end; it's too neat. Around 1900, the American writer O. Henry[85] wrote some eight hundred stories for magazines, all carefully and rather obviously structured. These can be entertaining in small doses, but soon start to feel formulaic and artificial. It is worth sampling O. Henry's tales as a lesson in skill—but also as a warning.

Short stories benefit from a very light structure that would be unsatisfactory in a novel. One of Chekhov's finest tales is *My Life*[86] which, as Craig Raine notes in an introduction, has been wrongly criticized as "deficient in shapeliness." Quite the contrary; in a short story, writes Raine, "obvious form is precisely to be avoided." Another well-known instance is *The Gold Fish* by R.B. Cunninghame Graham:[87] an eastern khalifa summons a famed athlete and gives him seven goldfish in a bowl, commanding him to run with these as a gift to the sultan. The athlete runs and runs for weeks and finally dies in the desert. That's it. There's little "development". You can't do things like that in a novel, but you can in a story.

7. Don't close it down. One of the many perils of formal structure in the story is that it encourages too tight a conclusion. Consider the Six-Word Story: this minimalist

---

[85] 1862–1910. His real name was William Sydney Porter. Collections of his stories are available in paperback editions, and there is a prestigious story prize given in his name.

[86] Reprinted with Raine's essay in *My Life and Other Stories*, in the Everyman's Library series.

[87] Reprinted in *The Devil and The Giro: Two Centuries of Scottish Stories* ed. Carl McDougall (1989). Joseph Conrad wrote to Graham: "Nothing I liked more since the gold-fish carrier story."

form was reputedly invented by Ernest Hemingway[88] who, one evening at the Algonquin café in New York, supposedly took a bet that he could produce a satisfactory story in six words; he won the bet with this:

— For sale: baby shoes. Never worn.

The strength of this lies in its open suggestiveness. I have sometimes set students to write six-word stories. Here are two products:

— Lottery win. Family squabbles. Burned it!
— "Too fast!" she screams. Ignore her.

The second of these is I think preferable, because it stimulates the imagination to go to work, whereas the Lottery win is all done and dusted, and the story closed down.

8. Tight time structure. As a rule, keep the time structure simple and compact. Flashbacks and jumps will be confusing and disruptive if you have no chance to re-orient your reader to another time, another place. Similarly, avoid back story. This is partly for reasons of space and economy, but also because of the need for intensity of experience—which is what short stories are all about. If you take the reader out of the present moment, you inevitably weaken that present.

A particular sub-species of the short story may be described as "the frozen moment." In this, a character is caught at a point of crisis in which they consider the circumstances which brought them to this. A recent example is Hanif Kureishi's *Weddings & Beheadings*.[89] A middle-eastern cameraman is waiting with his equipment to be collected for a job. He describes the horrific trade he has fallen into, filming weddings and terrorist beheadings. At the end, the doorbell rings …

---

[88] This episode may be apocryphal and there are problems with it: there is no record of the bet or its result anywhere in Hemingway's own writing, or anywhere else prior to c. 1990.

[89] Printed in *The National Short Story Prize* 2007. All the five finalist stories were read on BBC Radio 4 except for Kureishi's which was considered too sensitive at a time when a British journalist was being held hostage in Gaza.

9. Performance quality. Perhaps another aspect of the tight time structure I commend. It is valuable to think of a short story as something designed to be read aloud to an audience—even if you never actually do that. This emphasises the notion that a story is to be experienced in one go, snatched out of time.

10. Minimal information. "Art" said someone, "is life with the boring bits left out." Economy of information ought to be a feature of any fiction, but in the short story it is vital. Information is clutter. Ponder very carefully what the reader needs to know for the experience to work, and give no more than that. Consider the story told in the folk-song, *Sweet Polly Oliver*:

> When sweet Polly Oliver lay musing in bed,
> A sudden strange fancy came into her head:
> "Nor father nor mother shall make me false prove.
> I'll list for a soldier and follow my love."
> So early next morning she softly arose,
> And dressed herself up in her dead brother's
>   clothes.
> She cut her hair short and she dyed her face
>   brown,
> And went for a soldier in fair London town.
> Then up spoke the sergeant one day at their drill:
> "Oh, who's good for nursing? The captain he's ill."
> "I'm ready," said Polly. To nurse him she's gone,
> And finds it's her true love, all wasted and wan.
> The first week the doctor kept shaking his head.
> "No nursing can save him, young fellow," he said.
> But when Polly Oliver had nursed him back to life,
> He cried, "You have cherished him as if you were
>   his wife!"
> At that Polly Oliver she burst into tears,
> And told the good doctor her hopes and her fears,
> And very shortly afterwards, for better or for
>   worse,
> The captain took joyfully his pretty soldier nurse.

Notice the huge amount that we are *not* told: who is Polly Oliver? How old is she? Does she come from a working class or a middle class professional background? What is her mobile phone ring tone? Why did her brother die? What are his clothes like? What colour was the hair she cut short? Why do her parents object to her boyfriend? How does she get to London? What is wrong with her lover? The answer to all these questions is: we don't need to know. The story does not need this information. Look at your own writing and at all the information that you have given the reader: what is it for? What is your reason for giving us all that stuff? What is its justification?

But you may object: "That was just a song!" Certainly; and the short story arguably derives directly from the ballad. For economy in prose, look again at the tiny 49-word fable by Robert Louis Stevenson which we saw in Chapter Two, and notice all the things we are *not* told:

The Citizen and The Traveller

'Look round you,' said the citizen. 'This is the largest market in the world.'

'Surely not,' said the traveller.

'Well, perhaps not the largest,' said the citizen, 'but much the best.'

'You are certainly wrong there,' said the traveller.
    'I can tell you …'

They buried the stranger at dusk.

No names, no place names, no description, no explanation of the traveller's presence, no indication of how he met the citizen or of how he died. Actually, it is not even specified that either character is a man or a woman.

Such are my guiding principles for short stories. Many of them I have disobeyed myself; nonetheless, an awareness of these will help you consider how you go about writing stories, and also perhaps influence your reading of them.

WORK POINT: write some minimalist stories. There are various established formats: 6-words, or the 50-word "mini-saga", or the "39-er", and others, often referred to as "flash fiction". You choose, but write several. Compare the results and ask yourself why some work better than others. See if you can match Robert Louis Stevenson or Ernest Hemingway for dexterity.

16 Editing

"Writing is re-writing" goes the mantra. Innumerable authors are on record saying that the editing and re-writing of fiction is at least as important as the first draft. So: what does it involve?

Edit stages

Editing fiction tends to fall into these distinct phases:

1. A cooling-off period, after you've completed a first draft. For some writers this may require weeks if not months. You need this time to clear your head, and to look at your work afresh.
2. A broad edit, surveying the structure, the characters, the timescale, the general "fit" of the thing. Have you told the story as you wish? Is the pace right? Have you slowed it down with too much information? Have you varied it, with a rise and fall of action?
3. A fine edit, when you go through your text sentence by sentence.
4. Editing by your publisher, and then by their copy-editor, line by line.
5. Your re-examination of the text in the light of their recommendations.
6. Typesetting, and then proofreading.

At least, this is how it was in the Golden Age. Today, with changing technology, and with ever-tighter financial pressures on publishers (especially small publishers), these procedures are being truncated. But let's pretend …

The broad edit (1): Re-structuring

The broad edit may involve shifting entire sections of the work, so that you tell it in the order that is most effective, perhaps so that we enter the narrative at a different point. This is a difficult and delicate process. You may worry that the story is "not working", and respond in a panic by putting the climax in the middle and the coda at the beginning and cutting something else … with the result that the entire structure crumbles. Moreover, shifting blocks of narrative will certainly introduce new problems: things may no longer be clear, or congruent, or you may assume that the reader has some key piece of information which they no longer have— because you've shifted it to a position seventy pages later. The result of a re-jigging can be confusion and dismay.

Take it slowly. Be clear in your mind: what is this story about? What is the real issue here, the driving question? What is the effect that I am after? Only start re-structuring if it looks essential. And always keep clearly marked back-up copies of earlier versions, so that you can revert to these if need be.

Editing character at this stage is generally a matter of

- developing language and personality traits,
- achieving consistency, so that they are the same person throughout, even if they've learned hard lessons,
- ensuring that your character's motivations are clear, and that they tally with what happens.

The broad edit (2): Cutting content

Another familiar mantra: "Less is more". There are two aspects of this: economy of prose style (which we'll come to shortly), and economy of content. Many novels demonstrate that by *not* saying something, by implying an emotion, a danger, a moral dilemma, you may achieve more than by spelling it out. A good example occurs in Richard Hughes' *A High Wind In Jamaica*, concerning that group of white children captured in the Caribbean by a bunch of amiable and hapless pirates. One of the girls, Margaret, is slightly older than the others, and is passing puberty. The pirates are quite kind to the children, but find their presence on the pirate ship unsettling—in particular the presence of Margaret. One night the pirates get drunk, and come down the ladder to where the children are falling asleep. The sailors behave strangely; the captain's voice is altered: "There was a sort of suppressed excitement in it". But they are not the only ones:

> It was Margaret who had behaved most queerly. She had gone yellow as cheese, and her eyes large with terror. She was shivering from head to foot as if she had the fever. It was absurd. Then Emily remembered how stupidly frightened Margaret had been the very first night on the schooner.

On this occasion, nothing happens except that little Emily bites the captain's thumb. But a few days later, Margaret moves of her own accord into the captain's cabin, and will not speak to the younger children. Nothing more is said; there is no mention of any sex—but sexuality shimmers in the background of the novel from then on, unspoken and disturbing.

Cutting may include entire sections of your novel. It may be that one of your draft readers finds a whole chapter dull. So, do you need that chapter at all? Is it really there just as explanation of something (plot or character) that readers actually find perfectly obvious? If so, why not just cut it?

And remember that mantra: *Come in late, leave early*. A friend once sent me a draft of a novel which I much enjoyed except that it seemed to go on too long. I suggested major cuts to the final chapter, his publisher agreed—and the last thirty pages or so were simply dropped. The point of the story had been made; no need to say it again.

The fine edit (1): Take it carefully

Fine text editing can be a great pleasure, one of the most satisfying aspects of writing fiction. This is when you stop fretting over all those big doubts (*Have I got the structure right? Have I used the right point of view?*) and get down to the honest craft of honing words and refining your style.

It can be slow and exhausting work (I can generally edit no more than fifteen or sixteen pages in a day) and it must be done again and again (I edit most text four or five times). But unless you are very unlucky, your writing gets better with every minute that you spend upon it, and it shows.

Not everyone edits to the same extent. At one extreme there was Henry James who by some estimates tinkered with 90% of sentences between drafts. At the other was Georges Simenon—the prolific creator of the French detective Inspector Maigret—who claimed to do no revision whatever. In between are those Victorian writers like Dickens who were working to a tight periodical schedule (Dickens would write and deliver two thousand words to his publisher by lunchtime), and then others like Virginia Woolf who ran their own publishing houses and could take as long as they pleased. A search on the internet will find you images of manuscripts and typescripts with all the editions and corrections that their authors made; it is fascinating to look in careful detail at what they were doing, comparing the original sentence to see how it has been altered.

You will need to find the working procedure that is best for you. I do broad editing on the computer, where I can move things around readily. But later, for the fine edit, I have to print it out and make corrections on paper with a pencil: I need silence, and no tippy-tappy technology between me and the words. Other writers are happy with the computer throughout—though be careful: the lightning efficiency of computers has certain dangers. There is a story of a writer who finished a novel in which the protagonist was called David. At the last moment, the author decided to change this to Norman, and he used his computer's "find and replace" facility, making the alteration to the whole typescript in an instant. Unfortunately, he forgot that he had in the novel also referred to Michelangelo's statue of *David* ...

The fine edit (2): Economies of style

The early 20th century English novelist John Galsworthy once wrote that: 'To write well, even to write clearly, is a woundy business, long to learn, hard to learn, and no gift of the angels. Style should not obtrude between a writer and his reader.'

Galsworthy was contributing a foreword to a book by W.H. Hudson,[90] a novelist and naturalist. Hudson's novels are little read now, but his Patagonian memoir *Far Away And Long Ago* has many fans, helped by its luminously simple prose style. 'It is remarkably harmonious,' wrote Joseph Conrad, '… a sort of earnest quietness, absolutely fascinating … in the din of this age of blatant expression … It is as if some very fine, very gentle spirit were whispering to him the sentences he puts down on paper.'[91]

What does this mean? Above all: that style that calls attention to itself—"fine writing"—is frequently irritating and counterproductive; that readers in general hate to be told what to think or feel (which is what high style is often doing); that we want to consider the story and the characters, not the author's cleverness; and that taste usually shies away from rhetoric.

Chekhov's play *The Seagull* pits two authors against each other: there is Trigorin—older, successful, celebrated—and the younger Konstantin who is desperately ambitious but who knows in his heart that he will never match Trigorin's talent. Here is Konstantin examining their relative writing merits by considering an evocation of the night:

> My description of the moonlit night is overlong and overworked. Trigorin has worked out cunning little tactics, so for him it's no problem. He puts a broken bottle with its neck gleaming on the bank by the millpond, and then the black shadow of the waterwheel alongside it—and there you are, a moonlit night. I, meanwhile, have the glimmering light, the stars twinkling, a piano in the distance just audible in the fragrant stillness … It's ghastly![92]

---

[90] 1841–1922. Born and brought up in Argentina, Hudson lived much of his life in poverty in the south of England, and wrote his memoir in a boarding house while recovering from a serious illness.

[91] Joseph Conrad, letter to R.B. Cunninghame Graham, 2 June 1911.

[92] *The Seagull* (1896), Act Four (my trans.).

Trigorin's talent—and Konstantin's despair—is another instance of "Less is more". In other words, prose often works best when understated.

The leading 20th century exponent of this was Ernest Hemingway who propounded what came to be called the iceberg theory. He wrote: 'The dignity of movement of an iceberg is due to only one-eighth of it being above water.' Hemingway considered that only the facts should float above water; the emotional weight should be beneath the swell, unseen but massive. This led Hemingway to produce extremely bare, stripped-down "objective" prose which some writers have derided as incapable of carrying feeling at all (Saul Bellow mocked: 'Do you have emotions? Strangle them!').

What you must not do is weary your readers with redundant words.

Stripping away redundancies

I taught academic writing for a while at Dundee University. Academics can be bad at writing economically, and I would give students an exercise which required them to jettison from a given sentence as many redundant words as possible. For example:

> On the day that had been agreed for the commencement of manufacture, we received information indicating that the company had gone into administration.

That is twenty-three words. Why it should not be done in thirteen?

> The day manufacturing was to begin, we learned that the company was bankrupt.

Try this one:

> Our basic premise is that tangible facts should ideally be substituted for a range of opinions from all the various stakeholders.

That is twenty-one words. If you consider what the sentence is really trying to say—the nub of the matter—it comes down to four words: "Facts should replace opinions". If you think that some vital nuance has been lost—well, which vital nuance, exactly? When is a premise not "basic"? What is a "tangible fact"? What of any use does "all the various stakeholders" add?

In general, in editing any prose, I can cut it by at least ten to fifteen percent; whatever you are writing, this is a skill to cultivate. Twenty-two words reduced to fourteen is a cut of some 40%—which, if you managed it throughout your book, would be a cut from 100,000 words (perhaps 330 pages) to 60,000, or 200 pages.[93] If nothing else, you will have a grateful editor and probably grateful readers too—and you will have space to do other things in your story.

This process can be liberating, like parking a skip or dumpster in the street outside your house and filling it with unwanted chairs, shoes and kitchen utensils. One feels slimmer, lighter and healthier afterwards.

Norman Maclean's novella *A River Runs Through It* concerns a father raising his two sons in 1920s Montana, and teaching them to fly-fish—a skill that encapsulates the perfectionism and economy that Maclean saw as part of his Scots heritage. Both sons become writers. The film version[94] deftly conveys how the father sets the sons a writing task; the boys present their work and the father hands it back, saying only, "Half as long." The boys do that, and again the father reads it and only comments: "Half as long". And when they have done that, he says: "Good. Now throw it away"—for the important lesson has been learnt.

WORK POINT: an exercise in cutting.

---

[93] Assuming c. 300 words per page. Actual word rates vary considerably, of course.

[94] The 1992 film directed by Robert Redford had an outstanding script by Richard Friedenberg, for which he was nominated for an Oscar.

This is from an account by a woman revolutionary in Cuba:[95]

> Arturo addressed us in the wooden log hut, and one could hear the passion in his voice which made me feel the jungle somehow. He described his impressions of our leaders, and all the possible obstructions that could make progress difficult. I saw the sweat patches on his battledress, and the smell of sweat that was sweet and really quite pleasant because it seemed to evoke the hard lives of the poor rural labourers in our country's fields that we were hoping to liberate. As he spoke, his eyes ran over me. He took in my figure, his gaze like a warm stream purling through my silken black hair and over my full breasts and down the nape of my neck and back, to enclose my waist and my womanhood. He could not take his eyes off me. As he talked he was thinking of another sort of liberation—and my body began to respond, my bowels feeling loose and tumultuous, my flesh sensing that the situation was dangerous and full of risks …

That is 173 words long. The exercise is simple: cut it by half. Look for tautologies (phrases saying the same thing twice). Weed out the nonsensical and the non-sequitur, the vulgar, the wordy, the redundant, the embarrassing. Look for the tired cliché: replace it. What are you left with? Keep the result; we'll return to it.

Why *not* cut?

Before you get too carried away with your razor-blade, we should ask: is "less is more" always correct? George Eliot wasn't interested in writing sternly economical prose, nor was Henry James, nor Saul Bellow or William Styron, nor Salman Rushdie, Michel Faber or Kiran Desai today. Consider just once more the passage from Henry James's

---

[95] It's actually a parody of a book I was once sent to review.

The Portrait of A Lady concerning Isabel's sight of her husband with Madame Merle:

> Just beyond the threshold of the drawing-room she stopped short, the reason for her doing so being that she had received an impression. The impression had, in strictness, nothing unprecedented; but she felt it as something new, and the soundlessness of her step gave her time to take in the scene before she interrupted it.

Today, few authors would allow themselves such languid periods or so many words. It might be pruned to:

> She stopped outside the door; she had received an impression—nothing new, but it felt new. Her silent steps gave her time to absorb the scene before interrupting.

I've reduced fifty-five words to twenty-eight. James might retort, however, that his long sentences give us precisely what silence gives Isabel: the time to absorb the scene before we interrupt it. If your prose style can be justified, well and good. If not, work on it, and ensure that your style fits your subject; for example, is your imagery appropriate? Have you used metaphors or similes that have little connection with the world evoked? The Nigerian novelist Chinua Achebe uses very sparing description but his metaphors and similes are startlingly vivid. Writing about Ibo villages in West Africa,[96] he mentions huts with lamps inside so that the hut openings are like the eyes of a puma in the dark; and double rainbows which are like a mother and daughter, the one fresh and brightly coloured, the other faded.

Overcuts and damage

If you did the 'Cuban revolutionaries' exercise on cutting, you may have found yourself with a paragraph half the length of the original, perhaps even less. But now, look at it again: in the process of cutting, what have you lost? Are you now left with

---

[96] See *Things Fall Apart* (1958).

something characterless? Remember that this is first person narration: of whom do we get the stronger impression— Arturo or the woman speaking? The man to begin with, but she draws the focus onto herself, presenting herself as such a lovely specimen of sensual womanhood that Arturo cannot help but gaze at her. She is prefiguring a sexual relationship, and embodying in herself the erotic excitement of war and rebellion. If this is fiction, a novel in which she is the protagonist, it might be essential to convey these things. How would you edit the passage so as to preserve those aspects, while making it economical and readable? Try again.

Remember: editing is a process of cutting out that which is redundant, clichéd or inaccurate; it is *not* there to smooth away all the quirks and eccentricities that make prose vivid and supple. It is *not* there to remove all the fizz of the first draft, but to make it more accurate. One of Raymond Carver's collections of stories has the title *Would You Please Be Quiet, Please?* It is precisely the clumsy repetition that makes the phrase memorable.

Reading aloud

Editing is a slow process, in that you must consider your prose on several different levels: the words that make up each sentence; the sentences that neighbour each other in each paragraph; the overall style and vocabulary of the entire book.

For me, there is only one way to do this: read aloud. If you work in any other way, inevitably you will speed up. Your eye will start to skim, your brain will report what you *think* you have written—but that may not be what is on the page. Read aloud, and slowly, giving careful attention to the punctuation. Imagine that you are giving a formal lecture on the radio, and listen to your own text as you read. You must read slowly and clearly, because the audience cannot see you; they can only listen to your words, and need time to absorb each sentence. Read even more slowly than that; stop at the end of the sentence, and consider: does it say what it is supposed to say? Does the sentence actually make sense? Does it say anything idiotic? Is the vocabulary fresh, and the images sparkling—or do you repeat vocabulary that you have used nearby? Finally: *is each sentence interesting?* If it is not interesting, what excuse do you have for boring the poor reader who has paid good money for your book?

This is painstaking work. It is easy to relax, feel tired, let a few sentences go by … and then you lose what Martin Amis calls "the war against cliché".[97] It is frighteningly easy to make stupid mistakes: one of my novels went for typesetting with a woman wearing a green coat on one page which on the next page became a black coat—and this after I had checked the typescript more times than I can remember, and an editor had gone through it also. The procedure can be difficult: finding the right vocabulary *and* the right tone *and* avoiding repetition *and* an interesting rhythm is not easy. But it is real craft, and craft is satisfying. If you recall my notion that writing a book is analogous to fine cabinet-making: well, editing is when your French polish starts to glow.

Finding a friendly reader

At some stage before submitting professionally you will likely want to send the typescript out to a few friendly readers, to get an opinion. This is certainly valuable, but with some cautions:

- Wait until you are sure that your prose is in good shape. Don't tax a valued reader's patience by throwing early, poorly edited drafts at them.
- Choose your readers carefully. Don't waste time or paper on getting opinions from a dozen friends who are simply going to flatter you. This doesn't help anyone. You need a careful, considered and detailed response from people with a good understanding of fiction.
- Get more than one response. Don't depend on one opinion.
- Be careful when seeking opinions from other beginning writers. They *may* be good readers, but they may also be

---

[97] In his book of that name, 2001.

publishing. Lish took a minute interest in Carver's prose, to the extent that he re-wrote many of the stories. He changed titles, he changed the names of characters. He added in text of his own, while cutting large amounts of Carver's. When Lish received the typescript of a book of short stories called *Beginners,* he changed the title to *What We Talk About When We Talk About Love,* rewrote ten of the endings, and also cut around 50% of the words. In one case, Lish cut 78% of Carver's story.[99]

Raymond Carver was not at all happy with what was happening, although he was painfully torn, because he knew that he owed much of his success to Lish. Carver tried to stop the publication of *What We Talk About* ... but then changed his mind. Carver is today held up to students of creative writing as a model—but perhaps we should be praising his editor Gordon Lish instead.

Style and taste

Or should we be praising anyone? Ironically, some critics now blame Raymond Carver for having had too great an influence on creative writing; some students now believe Carver-esque minimalism to be the only style worth emulating. In a further twist, Carver himself was unhappy with the label. In a 1983 interview, Carver said: "There's something about 'minimalist' that smacks of smallness of vision and execution that I don't like". The lesson, surely, is: don't force yourself to write in a style with which you don't feel comfortable. Style is a matter of taste and fashion, nothing else. There are so many ways of writing: you should not feel obliged to follow any school.

Certain writers have laid down rules of literary taste, and rules for good prose. Leading the way recently has been Elmore Leonard, the American author of crime and cowboy novels, who decreed that one should never write prologues,

---

[99] The process can be examined in the Library of America edition of Carver's *Collected Stories* (2009) which prints the uncut version of *Beginners* together with the Lish version. You might care to Google "Carver Lish" to find articles on what happened.

should not open a book with a description of the weather (see above p. 118) and should never use adverbs in reporting speech—"Stop!" he cried *urgently*. Indeed, one should not use 'cried' either, when 'said' is quite sufficient, according to Leonard.

Such rules and regulations are easy to poke fun at; they are constricting and limiting and dull. But they contain a certain sound instinct: if your writing draws attention to its own clever style, finally you may make yourself look foolish. Elmore Leonard's own plain style has many admirers among more literary novelists.

Presentation

Before submitting a text to an agent or publisher, be sure to get the grammar, punctuation and formatting right (or at least, consistent). Few things irritate a reader—or an editor—more than a writer who has not bothered to learn how to punctuate. If you subvert the rules, be prepared to show why.

Buy yourself a "style guide", a book that sets out the conventions required by publishers; if you follow a guide produced by one of the major publishing houses, you cannot go far wrong. My own favourite is *New Hart's Rules* from Oxford University Press. This will tell you the correct use of semi-colons and commas, including the "Oxford comma" (you don't know the Oxford comma? Look it up). It will tell you when to put foreign words into italics, when to hyphenate, the difference between a preface and a foreword—and much else.

Books on creative writing usually conclude with a chapter on the process of submission to agents and publishers, including the physical presentation of typescripts. It seems unnecessary to reduplicate that information yet again here. My best advice is to obtain a copy of either *The Writers' Handbook* or *The Writers' and Artists' Year Book*. These include guidance on all aspects of getting published, as well as articles commenting on (for instance) the current state of the market for the various genres. They also include a directory of publishers and agents. The crucial thing is: read the instructions. Each agency and each publisher has their own submission procedures and requirements. Some are happy to receive text electronically; others will not even answer an email enquiry. If you haven't bothered to read their guidelines, you can't complain if they ignore you. There are also some useful websites giving practical advice. A good one to start with is www.writersservices.com

As to whether or not you need an agent: the debate is without end. I currently have four books in print, with various other projects coming to fruition. In every case, I have approached the publishers direct. But then, an agent (or the Society of Authors' legal department) has sorted out the deal afterwards.

Writing fiction is full of imponderables from start to finish. It can be a heartbreaking but also an exhilarating business. I wish you the very best of luck.

Index

Abouleila, Leila
  Minaret (2005), 114
accents, 178
  using punctuation, 179
act one, two, three. *See*
  structural elements
Adiga, Aravind
  The White Tiger (2008), 38
adventures. *See* stories
*Adventures of Baron
  Munchausen* (film, 1988),
  40
age. *See* character
agents, 220
Agus (Indonesian fisherman),
  16, 24
Almond, David
  Skellig, 131
Amis, Martin
  on cliché, 215
  Time's Arrow (1991), 87
anachronisms. *See* language
Atwood, Margaret
  The Handmaid's Tale
  (1985), 61
Auschwitz, 10, 18, 46, 85, 144,
  171–172
Austen, Jane, 5, 69
  editing of, 217
  Emma (1815), 109, 141
  Mansfield Park (1814), 81,
  108, 131
  Pride & Prejudice (1813),
  183
  Sense & Sensibility (1811),
  5, 56
autobiography, 23

Avatar (film, 2010), 32
*Awakening Conscience,
  The* (painting, 1853), 126

Ballard, J.G., 96, 197
Barker, Nicola
  Burley Cross Postbox Theft
  (2010), 35
Beckett, Samuel, 31
Bellow, Saul
  on Hemingway, 210
Benchley, Peter
  Jaws (1974), 55
Bennett, Arnold
  realist writing, 138
Besant, Walter, 89
Bible, language of. *See*
  landscape
Bierce, Ambrose
  *An Occurence At Owl Creek
  Bridge* (1891), 161
Bildungsroman. *See* novel
Blyton, Enid
  on character, 139
bookending. *See* structural
  elements
bookshops, 130
Borges, Jorge Luis, 31
  Fictions, 39
  On Rigor in Science (1946),
  90
Bowen, Elizabeth
  The Death of The Heart
  (1949), 119
Boyd, William
  Restless (2006), 104–105,
  166, 169

Brecht, Berthold
  Mother Courage (1941), 38
Breitenfeld, Battle of, 113
Brief Encounter (film, 1945), 11
Bronte, Emily
  Wuthering Heights (1847),
    36, 64, 85, 160
    dialogue in, 176
Brown, Dan
  The Da Vinci Code (2003),
    93, 138
Browning, Robert
  My Last Ducchess (1842), 62
  The Ring & The Book
    (1868–9), 33
buildings with history, 128
Burgess, Anthony
  A Clockwork Orange (1962),
    99
*Butch Cassidy & The Sundance
  Kid* (film, 1969), 148

Carey, Peter
  Oscar & Lucinda (1988), 56
Carpentier, Alejo, on magic
  realism, 39
Carver, Raymond, 197
  editing and style of, 217
  *Would You Please Be Quiet,
    Please?*, 214
Casablanca (film, 1942), 38, 49
  character build up, 147
  character traits, 144
  flashback, 165
  plot pacing, 159
  story elements, 83
  structure, 78
Casualty (BBC TV), 127
catalyst. *See* structural
  elements
Cervantes, Miguel de
  Don Quixote (1605–15), 38
Chandler, Raymond, 193
  Philip Marlowe, 136, 150
  The Big Sleep (1939), 60,
    131

chanson d'aventure (French
  poetry), 10, 12
character. *See also* stories
  acts of kindness, 147
  age, 136
  and conflict, 45
  arc, 9, 83
  build up, 132, 147
  changing, 8
  conflict, public *v.* private,
    52, 143
  conflicted, 48, 50, 56
  detectives, 54, 143
  dissatisfaction, 51
  distinctive traits, 55
  driving story, 46
  engaging with, 133
  Enid Blyton on, 139
  inventory, 136–137
  is fate, 45
  is plot, 45
  knowing your creations,
    135
  misfits, 12
  personal attributes, 136
  physical appearance, 138,
    144
  positioning description, 144
  public expectations, 53
  reacting, 46, 48, 83
  revealing moments, 149
  snap image, 139
  tags and motifs, 148
  tested, 48
  through dialogue, 175, *See
    also* language
  want *versus* need, 51
characters. *See* structural
  elements
Chaucer, Geoffrey, 89
  Troilus & Criseyde (c. 1385),
    145, 187, 193
  Wife of Bath's Prologue
    (c. 1395), 45
Chekhov, Anton
  My Life (1896), 87, 199

The Seagull (play, 1896), 209

Christie, Agatha, 65

climax. *See* structural elements

Clochemerle (G. Chevalier, 1934), 7

coda. *See* structural elements

codas in novels, 85

Coetzee, J.M.
  Summertime (2009), 26, 110, 115
  The Master of Petersburg (1994), 139
  Youth (2002), 26

Coleridge, S.T.
  on fancy and imagination, 152

Collins, Wilkie
  The Moonstone (1868), 33

complexity. *See* plot

Conan Doyle, Arthur
  The Hound of The Baskervilles (1902), 60, 103, 111, 120, 180

conflict. *See* character

Conrad, Joseph
  Heart of Darkness (1902), 32
  Lord Jim (1900), 51
  Nostromo (1904), 104, 188, 209
  Typhoon (1904), 109
  Victory (1915), 166

Conversation, The (film, 1974), 114

copy editor. *See* editing

Coronel, Battle of, 94

Crabbe, George
  Peter Grimes, 13

Crace, Jim
  attitude to research, 96
  Being Dead (1999), 96

Crumey, Andrew, 41

Culloden, Battle of, 113

Cunninghame Graham, R.B., 52
  The Gold Fish (1896), 199

cutting. *See* editing

Daniel, Frank, 6–7
  want *versus* need, 51–52

de Bernieres, Louis
  Birds Without Wings (2004), 40
  Captain Corelli's Mandolin (1994), 40
  The War of Don Emmanuel's Nether Parts (1990), 40

decisions, 83

Defoe, Daniel
  Robinson Crusoe (1719), 32

Derrida, Jacques, 135

dialogue, 175
  artificiality of, 181
  conveying information, 180
  doctor and HR officer, 177
  film, 182
  local characteristics, 180
  mannerisms in, 180
  real, 182

diaries. *See* novel

Diary of A Nobody, The (Grossmith, 1892), 35

Dickens, Charles, 69, 208
  David Copperfield (1850), 23, 28
  Great Expectations (1861), 129
  period detail, 90

distancing, 25

Donald, Jason
  Choke Chain (2009), 118

Donoghue, Emma
  Door (2010), 131

Dostoesvky, Fyodor
  Crime & Punishment (1866), 59

Durrell, Lawrence
  The Dark Labyrinth (1958), 130

dynamic writing, 4, 47–48, 112, 117, 125, 132, 137, 141–143, 152

Eco, Umberto, 41
   The Name of The Rose
      (1981), 130
economy in prose. *See* editing
editing
   copy editors, 216
   cutting, disadvantages, 212
   economy of effect, 208, 217
   economy of information,
      201
   finding a reader, 215
   presentation of text, 219
   reading aloud, 214
   stages of, 205
   stripping down prose, 210
   structure, 87
   style and taste, 218
Eliot, George, 69, 89
   Daniel Deronda (1871), 167
   Middlemarch (1871), 40, 52,
      69, 85–86
   period detail, 90
English Patient, The (film,
   1996), 186
entry point. *See* plot

Faber, Michel
   Fish (1998), 84
   Some Rain Must Fall (1998),
      170
   *The Crimson Petal & The
      White* (2002), 67, 71, 96,
      117, 177–178, 191
   Under The Skin (2000), 13
Falla, Jonathan
   Blue Poppies (2001), 94,
      108, 172, 188
      Tibetan landscape in,
         105
   Glenfarron (2008), 189
   Poor Mercy (2005), 25, 42,
      135, 149, 152
family epic. *See* novel
Farrell, J.G.
   The Siege of Krishnapur
      (1973), 85

fate. *See* character
film & fiction, 185
   authors of, 193
   camerawork, 187
   panoramic shot, 188
   spy cameras, 189
   still shots, 192
film/fiction overlaps, 185
finding stories, 13
flashback. *See* structural
   elements
Flaubert, Gustave
   Madame Bovary (1857),
      46, 51, 63, 85, 143, 147,
      149, 163
   Sentimental Education
      (1864), 36
foreshadowing. *See* plot
Forster, E.M.
   A Passage To India (1924),
      109
   Aspects of The Novel (1927),
      155
   on plot, 155
Fowles, John
   the Collector (1963), 131
   *The French Lieutenant's
      Woman* (1969), 171
Frayn, Michael, 41
   Spies (2002), 162
Freeling, Nicolas
   Gun Before Butter (1963),
      126, 156–157
   oaths in, 179
   plot and question, 156
   Van der Valk, 54

Galsworthy, John
   on writing well, 209
Garland, Alex
   The Beach (2007), 32
Gautreaux, Tim
   *The Pine Oil Writers'
      Conference* (2010), 198
Gawain & The Green Knight
   (late 14th c.), 47, 77

glossaries, 179
Goethe, J.W. von
    Wilhelm Meister's
        Apprenticeship
        (1794), 36
Golding, William
    Lord of The Flies (1954),
        32, 53
    Rites of Passage (1980),
        8, 109
Gone With The Wind (film,
    1939), 186
Gordimer, Nadine
    My Son's Story (1990), 115
    The Pickup (2001), 81, 83,
        159
Greene, Graham, 193
    Dr Fischer of Geneva
        (1980), 170
    The Quiet American (1955),
        13
Grimmelshausen, J. von
    Simplicissimus (1668), 37
    The Life of Courage (1670),
        37
Gulliver's Travels (Swift, 1726),
    32

Hamid, Mohsin
    The Reluctant
        Fundamentalist (2007),
        56, 64, 165
Hamlet (Shakespeare, 1600), 20
Hardy, Thomas
    Far From The Madding
        Crowd (1874), 49
    Jude The Obscure (1895),
        13, 51, 96, 115
        Biblical landscape in,
            107
    Tess of The D'Urbervilles
        (1891), 51, 105
    The Return of The Native
        (1876), 104, 188
Hartley, L.P.
    The Go-Between (1953), 162

Hemingway, Ernest, 70
    iceberg theory, 210
    prose style, 217
    six-word story, 200
    The Old Man & The Sea
        (1952), 109
Henry, O
    short stories of, 199
historical epic. *See* novel
Hitchcock, Alfred
    McGuffins, 7
    North By Northwest (film,
        1959), 7
Hitler, Adolf
    plot to kill, 170
Hollywood, 81, 83
Holman Hunt, William
    (painter), 126
Hudson, W.H.
    Far Away & Long Ago
        (1918), 209
Hughes, Richard
    A High Wind In Jamaica
        (1929), 53, 63, 140, 206

iceberg theory. *See*
    Hemingway, Ernest
Iliad, The (Homer), 6
inciting incident. *See* structural
    elements
Inspector Morse, 149
interior description, 123
    attic, cellar, kitchen, 131
    sounds & smells, 127
inventory of attributes. *See*
    character

James, Henry
    plot question, 157
    social attitudes in, 91
    The Art of Fiction (1888),
        46, 89
    The Awkward Age (1899),
        136
    The Portrait of A Lady
        (1881), 91, 192, 213

The Wings of The Dove
(1902), 8–9, 46, 151, 157
Jansson, Tove
*The Exploits of
Moominpappa* (1949),
28
Jaws (film, 1975), 55
journeys. *See* stories, *See also*
novel
Joyce, James, 31
Portrait of The Artist
(1916), 37
Jungle Is Neutral, The (Spencer
Chapman, 1949), 108

Kadare, Ismail
The Successor (2003), 33
Kelman, James
How Late It Was, How Late
(1994), 62
speech in, 179
Kennedy, A.L.
*Night Geometry & The
Garscadden Trains*
(1990), 62
Kesey, Ken
*One Flew Over The Cuckoo's
Nest* (1964), 13
kindness, acts of. *See* character
King Lear (Shakespeare, 1605),
84
Knights, L.C.
*How many children had
Lady Macbeth?*, 136
Kundera, Milan
Ignorance (2002), 50
*The Unbearable Lightness of
Being* (1984), 50
Kureishi, Hanif
Weddings & Beheadings
(2007), 200
Kurosawa, Akira
Rashomon (film, 1950), 32

L.A. Confidential (film, 1998),
186

labyrinths, 130
Lampedusa, Giuseppe de
The Leopard (1961), 142
landscape, 103
and emotion, 105
and mood, 103
as situation, 108
Biblical (in Hardy), 107
changing, 112
choice of, 108
human resonance, 110
picnics, 109
scents and sounds, 112
symbolic force of, 108
language
anachronisms, 99
invented, 99
of professions, 99
period, 98
register, 150, *See also*
research
Larsson, Steig
*The Girl With The Dragon
Tattoo* (2005), 54, 131,
143
Lawrence, D.H.
Sons & Lovers (1913), 37
le Carré, John
speech mannerisms in, 179
The Secret Pilgrim (1991),
41
*The Spy That Came In From
The Cold* (1963), 131
The Tailor of Panama
(1996)
accent in, 150
speech register in, 176
Leonard, Elmore
rules for writers, 118, 218
Lessing, Doris, 197
libraries, 130
Life Is Beautiful (film, 1997),
46
limited omniscience. *See* voice,
third person
Lindsay, Joan

Picnic At Hanging Rock
(1967), 109
Lish, Gordon
and Raymond Carver, 217
Lost Horizon (film, 1937), 32
Love, Actually (film, 2003), 41
lying, 24

Maclean, Norman
*A River Runs Through
It* (1975), 27, 62, 211
magic realism. *See* novel
Mann, Thomas
as scriptwriter, 193
The Magic Mountain
(1924), 37
Marquez, Gabriel Garcia
*Chronicle of A Death
Foretold* (1981), 158
*One Hundred Years of
Solitude* (1967), 39, 161
Marshall, James V.
Walkabout (1971), 109
Maugham, W.S., 197
Collected Stories preface
(1951), 61
The Vessel of Wrath (1931),
95
Three Fat Ladies of Antibes
(1951), 13
Maupassant, Guy de
On The Water (1888), 119
McEwan, Ian
Enduring Love (1997), 99,
177
On Chesil Beach (2007), 49
McGuffins. *See* Hitchcock,
Alfred
Meek, James
The People's Act of Love
(2005), 8
Melville, Herman
Moby-Dick (1851), 109
Melville, Hermann
Billy Budd (1924), 13
men described, 138

Mercier, Pascal
Night Train To Lisbon
(2004), 8, 11, 51, 129,
131, 145
misery memoirs, 29
misfits. *See* stories
*Miss Smilla's Feeling
For Snow* (Hoeg, 1992),
118
Mitchell, Margaret
Gone With The Wind
(1937), 186
Moggach, Deborah, 45
on character, 135
screenplays, 183
Tulip Fever (1999), 85
Molina, Antonio Munoz
Sepharad (2001), 42, 66
Moore, Lorrie
BBC interview, 94, 118
moral dilemmas, 18
Morecombe and Wise
(comedians), 56
multiple threads, 167
mysteries. *See* plot

Nabokov, Vladimir, 94
narrator. *See* voice
dead, 60, 62
New Hart's Rules (2005), 219
Nicholson, William
career, 193
*The Secret Intensity of
Everyday Life* (2010), 40,
86, 167
novel
Bildungsroman, 36, 86
diary, 35
epistolary, 34
family epic, 39
historical epic, 38
journey, 32
magic realism, 39
panoramic chronicle, 40
picaresque, 37, 86
Rashomon type, 32

objectivity. *See* voice, third person
O'Flynn, Catherine
    What Was Lost (2007), 116, 125, 191
omniscience. *See* voice, third person
On The Shore (virtual novel), 59, 65–66, 68, 138, 144, 150, 170
Ondaatje, Michael
    The English Patient (1992), 186
openings, 27
Oscar-winning films, 186

pacing. *See* plot
Pamuk, Orhan
    My Name Is Red (1998), 60, 157–159
    plot question, 158
    Snow (2002), 118
    The Museum of Innocence (2010), 10, 49, 64, 81, 129, 130, 172
panorama. *See* novel
Pasternak, Boris
    Dr Zhivago (1957), 8–9, 167
Pears, Iain
    An Instance of The Fingerpost (2000), 33, 66, 168
    The Dream of Scipio (2003), 168
period detail, 90, *See also* language
physical appearence. *See* character
picaresque. *See* novel
picnics. *See* landscape
pitching, 20
planning, 1
plot, 75, 155, 164, *See also* structural elements
    complexity is arbitrary, 157
    entry point, 160

foreshadowing, 171–172
multiple threads, 168
mysteries, 155
pacing information, 158, 169
raisonneur, 166
revealing truth backwards, 163
shocks, 169
subplot, 86, 166
subplot and theme, 165
what is the question?, 156
point of view, 59
Polti, Georges
    The Thirty Six Dramatic Situations (1924), 5
Powell, Anthony
    Books Do Furnish A Room (1971), 149
presentation of text. *See* editing
Pritchett, V.S.
    on short story writing, 197
professions. *See* language
Proulx, Annie, 197, 70
    The Hellhole (2004), 39

question. *See* structural elements

Raine, Craig
    on Chekhov, 199
raisonneur (commentator), 166
Rankin, Ian
    Rebus, 54
    The Falls (2001), 181
Rashomon (film, 1950). *See* stories
reading aloud. *See* editing
Rear Window (film, 1954), 41
register. *See* language
Rendell, Ruth (as Barbara Vine)
    The Minotaur (2005), 130
Rescued By Fido, 167
research, 89
    digging for truffles, 93

errors of fact, 93
fictional and invented, 96
purpose of, 89
social attitudes, 91
specialities, 98
speech & language, 98
resolution. *See* structural
elements
revealing moments. *See*
character
reversal. *See* structural
elements
Richardson, Samuel
Clarissa Harlowe (1748), 34
Pamela (1740), 34
Sir Charles Grandison
(1753)
preface, 34
Riviere, William
Echoes of War (1997), 27, 39
Kate Caterina (2001), 56,
151, 129, 163–164
rules for writers. *See* Leonard,
Elmore

Saki (H.H. Munro), 124
Salinger, J.D.
The Catcher In The Rye
(1951), 28
Schaefer, Jack
Shane (1949), 51, 188
Schlink, Bernhard
The Reader (1995), 57
Sebald, W.G., 42
Austerlitz (2001), 31
Seger, Linda
The Art of Adaptation
(1992), 24
sensory information, 112, 127
sequence. *See* structural
elements
Shakespeare, William
fights in, 92
Short Cuts (film, 1993), 186
short stories, 197
market for, 197

six-word stories, 199
show, don't tell, 149, 194
Simenon, Georges, 208
Simmel, Georg
The Adventure (1911), 10,
32, 160
Snow Falling On Cedars
(Guterson, 1996), 118
social attitudes. *See* research
Some Like It Hot (film, 1959),
148
speech. *See* language, dialogue
step outline, 81
Sterne, Laurence
Tristram Shandy (1759–67),
28
Stevenson, Robert Louis
Dr Jekyll & Mr Hyde (1886),
49
The Citizen & The Traveller
(1887), 12, 86, 202
Treasure Island (1883), 28
stories
adventures, 10, 32
autobiography, 23
essential elements, 5–6, 16
family, 14, 39
identifying, 5
journeys, 8
misfits, 12, 115
moral dilemmas, 18
past catching up, 51, 52
Rashomon type, 66, 168
storybooks (types), 31
stream of consciousness, 65
structural elements. *See also*
plot
act one, 76, 78, 158
act three, 77, 159
act two, 79, 159
bookending, 162
catalyst, 76–77
characters, 76
climax, 77–78
coda, 77, 84
flashback, 79, 164

inciting incident, 76–77
question, 79, 156, 160
resolution, 77
scene, 159
sequence, 76–78, 159
time frame, 160
turning point, 76
twist, 77, 170
world, 76–78, 84
structure, 31, 75
three-act, 75, 81, 83, 86, 156, 158, 164, 185
style and taste, 218
style guides, 219
Styron, William
Sophie's Choice (1979), 10, 18, 85, 114, 120, 144, 147, 171–172
subplot. *See* plot
Szabo, Magda
The Door (1987), 171

tags and motifs. *See* character
Tennessee Screenwriting Association
Twenty Basic Plots, 6
tense, 71
past, 72
present, 71
present continuous, 71
present perfect, 72
theme, 83
Third Man, The (film, 1949), 186
thirty six plots, 5
threads, multiple. *See* plot
time frame. *See* structural elements
Tolstoy, Leo, 13
Anna Karenina (1873–7), 14, 141, 165, 167
War & Peace (1863–9), 38, 89, 96
townscape, 103, 113
as "character", 116
human detail, 114

social distinctions, 115
sounds and smells, 114
train hijack, Netherlands, 95
trolley problems, 18
Trollope, Anthony, 40
truffles. *See* research
turning point. *See* structural elements

Vargas Llosa, Mario
A Writer's Reality (1988), 25
Vincent (Irish boy), 14, 24
voice
first person, 59
first person framing, 63
second person, 66
third person, 68, 151

want *versus* need, 51, 137
weather, 103, 118
websites
BBC Writersroom, 183
Hotel San Clemente (Venice), 128
Internet Archive (Polti), 5
Tate Online, 126
The Daily Script, 183
Writers Services, 220
Wells, H.G.
The Country of The Blind (1911), 32
The First Men In The Moon (1901), 32
Welsh, Irvine
speech in, 179
Trainspotting (1993), 41
West Side Story (musical, 1957), 92
Wharton, Edith
The Reef (1912), 148
White, Edmund
Times Literary Supplement essay, 90, 92
White, Patrick
A Fringe of Leaves (1976), 8

Riders In The Chariot
    (1961), 13
Voss (1957), 38
Wilder, Thornton
    The Bridge of San Luis Rey
        (1927), 161
women described, 140
Woolf, Virginia, 31, 65, 138,
    208
work points, 4–5, 8, 12, 14,
    16, 20, 32, 35, 47–48, 55,
    68, 71–72, 78, 81, 84, 98,
    100, 105, 112–113, 116,
    126–128, 130, 132, 137, 145,
    158, 162, 164, 173, 178, 182,
    184, 203, 212

world. *See* structural elements
write what you know, 23, 89
Writers' Handbook, The, 219

Zafon, Carlos Ruiz
    The Shadow of The Wind
        (2001), 131

Writing Science Fiction 'What if…!'

Who else wants to write science fiction?
Written by professional writer (see www.lazette.net/) this book takes the reader by the hand and explains exactly how to create a commercially successful science fiction novel. The author is well known in the genre and regularly teaches creative writing. This book defines science fiction and explains the different categories of science fiction. The reader is then taught the basics of research, how to build a world based on science and myth, how to build 'the others', namely building up believable characters in your Aliens, how to write the language of the future, placing stories in the universe, space travel, the possibilities of government in the future, the challenge of writing something new, creating an effective outline, being a professional writer and preparing your manuscript for the publisher.

Lazette Gifford is a name in science fiction circles. She lives with her husband and family in the USA where she is a prolific writer, photographer and computer generated artist.

Author Lazette Gifford | **Price** £10.99 €12.99 | **Format** Paperback, 215 x 135mm, 160pp

ISBN 978-1-84285-060-2

Kate Walker's 12 Point Guide to Writing Romance

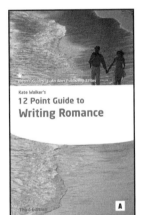

Here is how to become a published romance writer
If you want to write romance and be a professional writer then this book is a must for you. Following on from the success of the first edition of this book, which won a major award, this guide explains what is meant by romance and takes you through the process of writing emotion and conflict. The author explains how dialogue should be natural between your heroine and her hero and she explains the difference between sensuality and passion. With an expanded text and more true insider-secrets this is a must for all writers of romance, whether professional or amateur.
In this book you will learn:
• How to write emotion and create PTQ (page turning quality).
• Why dialogue is the lifeblood of your novel.
• The importance of 'after'.
• Why the intense black moment is so important.

Kate Walker has published in over 50 countries and has sold over 15 million romance novels worldwide.

Author Kate Walker | **Price** £10.99 €12.99 | **Format** Paperback, 215 x 135mm, 160pp

ISBN 978-1-84285-128-9

Writing Historical Fiction -

Creating the historical blockbuster
Who else wants to become a top selling novelist?
Have you always wanted to write historical fiction but not known
how to go about it? Or are you a published novelist who wants to
switch genres? In her meticulously researched book – packed with
worked examples, summaries and tips - Marina Oliver covers all
aspects of writing historical fiction –
This book includes details on:
• ten things you need to do to get started
• how to research your target period
• presenting your work to a publisher or agent
• the 5 stages of a plot
• how to write convincing dialogue
• the publication process

Marina Oliver has published over 50 historical novels and is a well-
known teacher of creative writing.

Author Marina Oliver | **Foreword** Richard Lee Founder of the Historical Novel Society
Price £10.99 €12.99 | **Format** Paperback, 215 x 135mm, 160pp

ISBN 978-1-84285-077-0

Writing 'how-to' articles and books

How to share your know-how and get published
Here is how to be a successful non-fiction writer
Who else wants to use their knowledge and experience to write non-
fiction articles and books?
It really could be you! Just imagine, with a little bit of guidance you
really could have your book on the bookshelves of national and even
international chains of bookshops. This book will show you how to
achieve it.
In this book Chris McCallum explains how to:
• Assess your knowledge and experience.
• Write 'how-to' articles.
• Write for magazines.
• Survive and succeed in today's publishing world.
• Break in with tips and fillers.
• Approach your market.
• Write a 'how-to' book.

Chriss Mc Callum has over 30 years of experience in the book trade both as a writer and as a publishing
executive.

Author Chriss McCallum | **Price** £10.99 €12.99 | **Format** Paperback, 215 x 135mm, 240pp

ISBN 13 978-1-84285-095-4

Writing Crime Fiction -

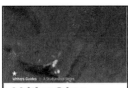

Making Crime Pay
Information Points
• Written by an expert who is a published crime writer
• Deals with a growing market of amateurs and undergraduates
• Each chapter develops a mental or practical skill
• Advice packaged in bite-sized chunks.

Here is how to become a published crime writer
Writing crime is an excellent introduction to
the genre from a well-established and
highly respected author.

In this book you will learn:
• How to start writing crime
• How to layer your novel with clues
• How to find a market for your work
• How to be a professional crime writer

Foreword by
International
Best-selling author
Val McDermid

Janet Laurence is an established crime writer. She is the author of the *Darina Lisle* crime series and the *Canaletto* murder series and the novel *To Kill the Past*. She is also the writer in residence at a college in Australia every summer. Janet Laurence lives in Somerset where like her heroine she enjoys cooking.

Author Janet Laurence | **Price** £10.99 €12.99 | **Format** Paperback, 215 x 135mm, 160pp

ISBN 13 978-1-84285-088-6

Starting to Write: Step-by-step guidance to becoming an author

Information Points
• Written by an expert academic who is also a published writer
• Deals with a growing market of amateurs and undergraduates
• Each chapter develops a mental or practical skill
• Advice packaged in bite-sized chunks.

Here is how to become a published writer
Many people yearn to become a published writer but publishers complain of the poor quality manuscripts they receive and how they are un-publishable. There are a substantial number of novice writers who are making totally avoidable mistakes.
In this book you will learn:
• How to start writing and become your best critic
• How to deal with writers block, rejection and still keep writing
• How to find a market for your work
• How to find the best writing style and best area to write in, for your personality.

Chriss Mc Callum has over 30 years of experience in the book trade both as a writer and as a publishing executive.

Author Dr Rennie Parker | **Price** £10.99 €12.99 | **Format** Paperback, 215 x 135mm, 160pp

ISBN 978-184285-093-0